FASHION DESIGN
DRAWING COURSE

REVISED AND UPDATED SECOND EDITION

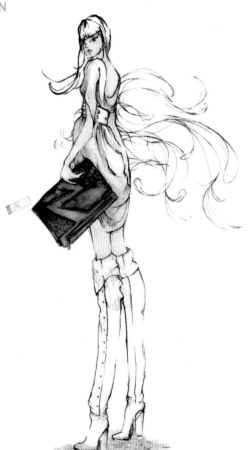

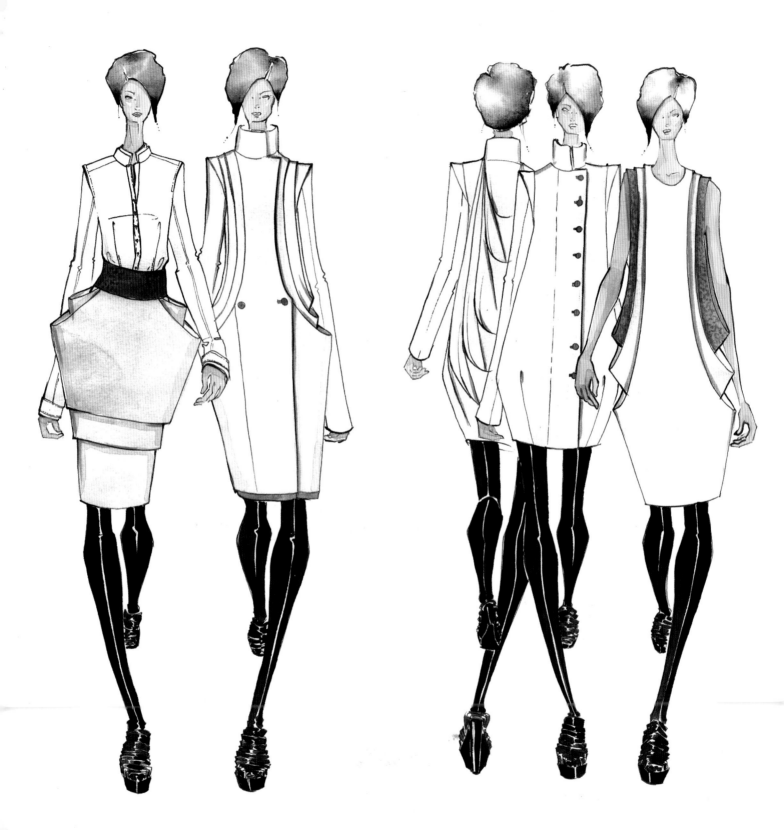

FASHION DESIGN
DRAWING COURSE
REVISED AND UPDATED SECOND EDITION

Principles, practices, and techniques: the new guide for
aspiring fashion artists—**now with digital art techniques**

Caroline Tatham & Julian Seaman
Revised edition: **Jemi Armstrong & Wynn Armstrong**

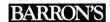

A QUARTO BOOK

First edition for North America published in
2011 by Barron's Educational Series, Inc.

All inquiries should be addressed to:
Barron's Educational Series, Inc.
250 Wireless Boulevard
Hauppauge, NY 11788
www.barronseduc.com

ISBN: 978-0-7641-4730-2
Library of Congress Control Number:
2010940956
QUAR.FDC2

Conceived, designed, and produced by
Quarto Publishing plc
The Old Brewery
6 Blundell Street
London N7 9BH

Senior editors: Lindsay Kaubi,
    Chloe Todd Fordham
Digital co-author: Sha Tahmasebi
Art editor: Emma Clayton
Designer: Anna Plucinska
Photographer: Phil Wilkins
Art director: Caroline Guest
Creative director: Moira Clinch
Publisher: Paul Carslake

Color separation in China by PICA
International Pte Ltd

Printed by 1010 Printing International
Ltd., China

9 8 7 6 5 4 3 2 1

Contents

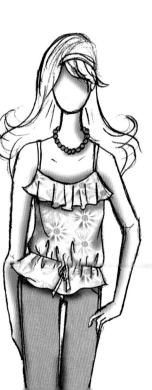

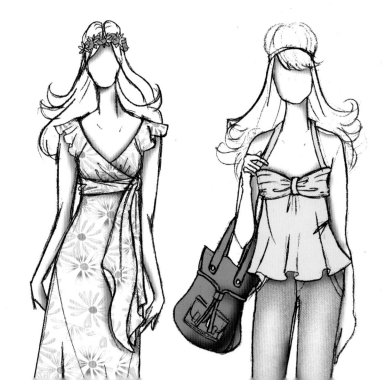

Introduction

Fashion is, by its very nature, an ever-changing art. Oscar Wilde remarked that "Fashion is a form of ugliness so intolerable that we have to alter it every six months," but it is this continual evolution, the constant reinvention of old trends and the creation of new ones, that lends the fashion industry its excitement and glamour.

This book is aimed at aspiring fashion designers and illustrators, and anyone with an interest in the fascinating world of style. The book is modeled around the fashion courses offered by colleges and universities, with twenty-seven units each containing a project to lead you step by step through the process of illustrating terrific designs. You don't need to know all about the big fashion names to take this course, nor do you need to be a genius with a paintbrush or sewing machine. The aim of this book is to unravel the mystique surrounding fashion, and to show how designs can be created through a systematic process of research and development, and the use of a range of illustration techniques. All you need to begin is enthusiasm and a willingness to express your own unique view of the world.

In the first chapter, "Finding inspiration," you will learn that creating a design is not a mystical affair but simply about researching, developing, and reinventing an inspiring theme. If you look at your surroundings through the eyes of a designer, you will see that inspiration is everywhere—museums, art galleries, the seashore, the city streets, even your familiar home and garden can provide you with raw material. This chapter will show you how to identify and research a source of inspiration, and how to use this inspiration

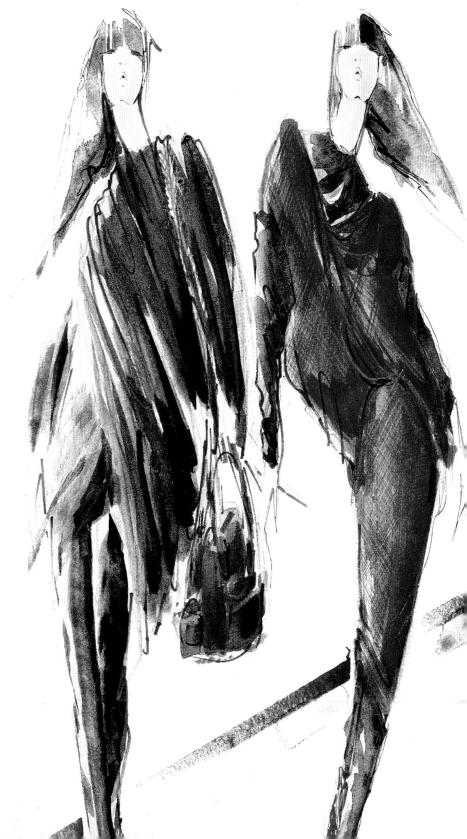

▶ **CAPTURE THE POSE**
Trying to capture a realistic pose in your illustrations can help to show how the fabric will behave when shaped into a garment.

to guide your designs, through the use of mood boards for example. It will also give some suggestions about how to put your own special spin on an idea, perhaps by enlarging scale to explore the unseen details of an ordinary object, or by bringing the patterns and shapes of a painting or a building into a new context, or by using your source to inspire a fabric design that will be the focus of the garment.

Once you have developed some great design ideas, you need to be able to represent them on the page. The second chapter, "Illustrating fashion," will give you the confidence to expand your drawing technique to include methods such as collage and mixed media. A mistake students often make is to believe they must develop a personal drawing style early on, and then stick to it. This book encourages plenty of experimentation—if you keep pushing the boundaries, your ideas will always be fresh. Experiments don't always work, of course, but you must have the courage to fail—this is part of the learning process.

One important point to keep in mind while working through this course is that the final aim of any fashion design is to produce a real garment that can be worn on a real human body. An article of clothing drawn on a figure that is wildly out of proportion will lack authority because no one will be able to imagine actually wearing it. The second chapter therefore explains an easy paper-folding method that an inexperienced designer can use as a guide for creating fashion figures. During this part of the course, you will learn to observe carefully and to hone your representational skills, as you practice drawing people and garments from life. You will also learn how to be bold in your designs, filling each page with drawings that show conviction.

The third chapter, "Planning and designing," takes your design work into the wider context of the fashion industry. Being a successful designer is not about producing flamboyant one-off pieces, but about

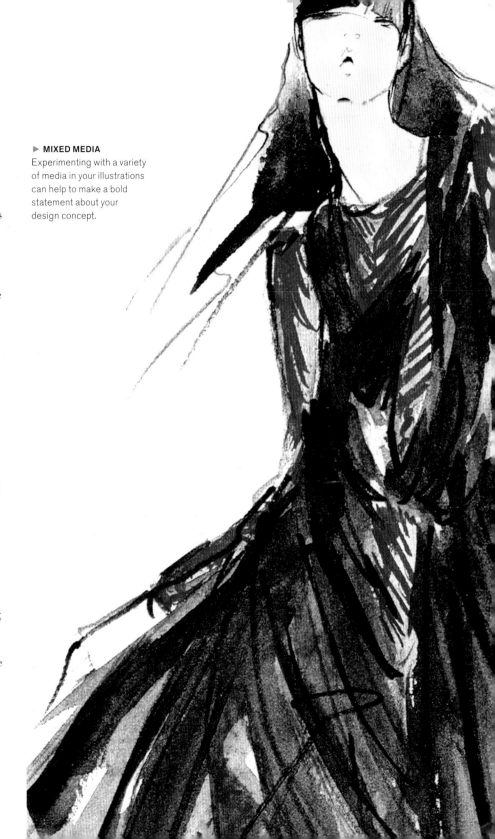

► **MIXED MEDIA**
Experimenting with a variety of media in your illustrations can help to make a bold statement about your design concept.

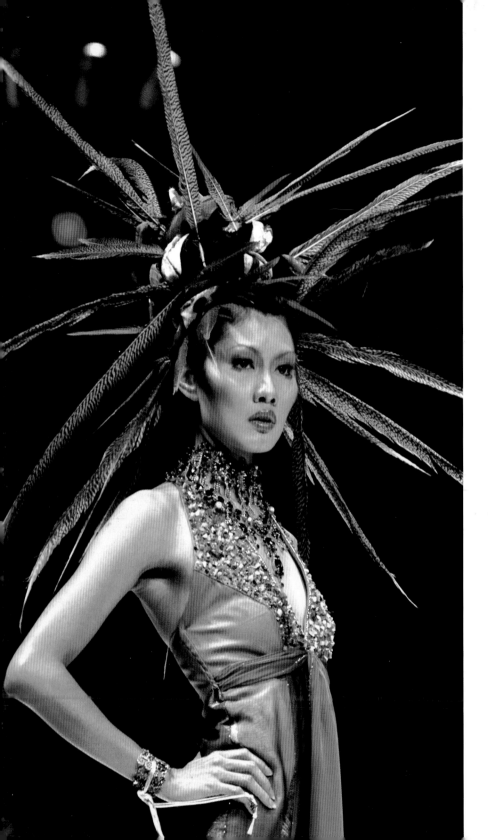

developing your inspiration into a cohesive range of designs that share a strong look, while offering as much choice to the customer as possible. This chapter will teach you how to work to a brief, to take into account considerations such as budget and seasonal requirements, and to build a collection aimed at a target customer whose tastes you might well not share yourself.

The final chapter, "Communicating your vision," looks at how all these wonderful ideas can be best shown off to colleagues, tutors, employers, and clients. When it comes to presenting your concepts, remember that clarity is key—there is no point in creating superb designs if no one can understand the illustrations. This chapter explains how to support your creative illustrations with flat working drawings and how to build a professional-looking presentation board. It also shows how every aspect of the presentation—from the style of drawing to the poses of the figures—can work together to communicate your vision with maximum impact.

Working through this book will give you the tools you need to create and illustrate designs, as well as the confidence to set off on your career as a fashion designer. Your most important assets are an open mind and a pair of fresh eyes; and remember, as you venture into this highly competitive yet rewarding business, fashion design should above all be fun.

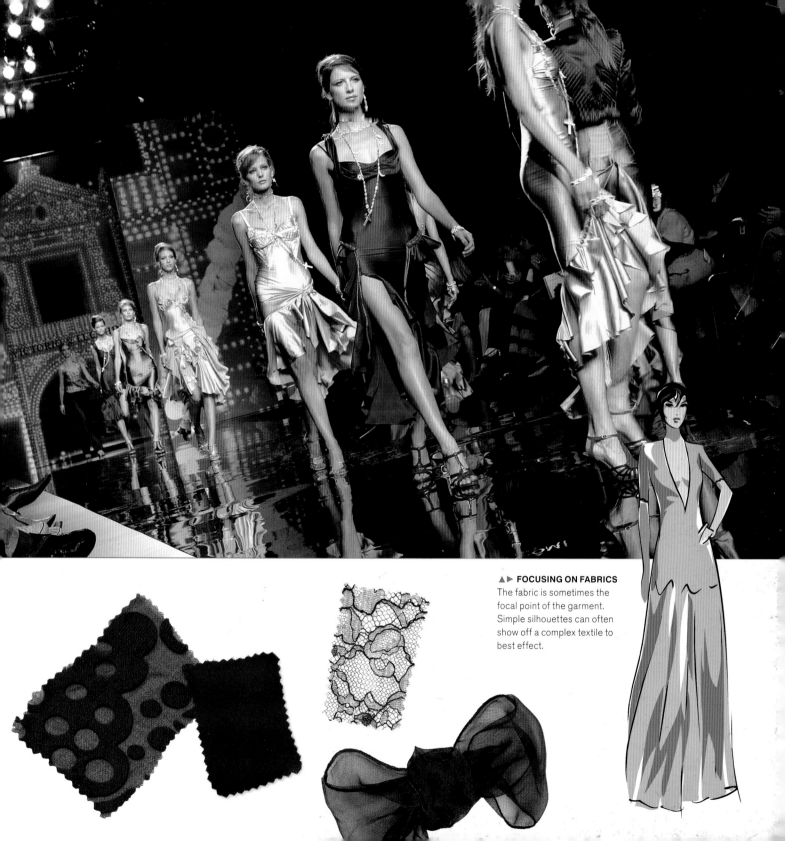

▲▶ FOCUSING ON FABRICS
The fabric is sometimes the focal point of the garment. Simple silhouettes can often show off a complex textile to best effect.

About this book

Following the format of a college course, this book is organized into units, each one looking at an aspect of the illustration of fashion design. The units are grouped into four chapters, so you progress logically from finding inspiration to using illustration techniques to planning a collection to presenting your ideas. Throughout the book, "inspiration files" provide background information on topics approached in the units.

Inspiration files

Periodically, "inspiration files" are included that provide background inspiration on the topics in the chapters.

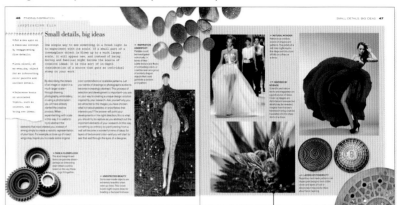

Illustrations show examples of images that could inspire fashion design; the captions suggest how.

Units

Each unit has a different topic as its focus, with a general introduction to that topic. Central to each unit is a project that sets a specific challenge.

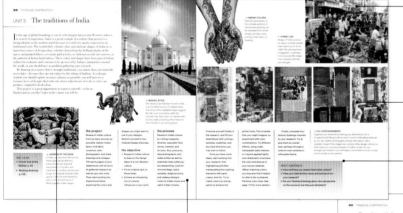

Topics and associated projects are explored using a range of visuals.

Pages from designers' sketchbooks show how ideas are developed.

The self-critique questions will help you assess your own work.

Most of the units run for four pages. Each unit contains "the project," a brief statement of the task, "the objective," a summary of its aims, and a "self-critique" section of questions to use when assessing the results.

The "process" provides a step-by-step guide to completing the project.

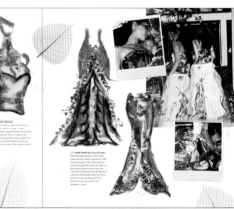

On the follow-on pages, illustrations by other designers suggest ways in which you might approach the topic.

Assessing your work

Whether you are a student enrolled in a course or simply working through this book on your own at home, it is essential to keep reviewing your working practice. You will not progress unless you look at your work critically, assessing whether you have achieved what you set out to do.

When you start to be artistically creative, it is often difficult to judge whether what you have done is any good. Oddly, what tends to happen is that students are far too self-critical and fail to spot when they are on to a winning idea. It is always worth pursuing something that you know works for you. However, you also need to be able to ruthlessly filter out the ideas that are not working. At first, you may lean heavily on the opinion of people such as tutors, but there will come a time when you know enough about yourself and your designs to select for yourself what works and what doesn't.

In this book, you are asked to carry out a self-critique on each project. Don't be too hard on yourself, but think honestly about whether your work has succeeded in the ways indicated by the questions. Here are some tips to help you with your self-assessment:

- Much of the design process has to do with self-discipline, so judge your work honestly. You should work freely and treasure your rough ideas (they are often more exciting than an overworked concept), but you need to know which ones to reject.

- Show your work to family and friends, and accept their compliments. The most experienced designers still need to feel their efforts are appreciated. Even a throwaway comment from a friend such as, "I couldn't have drawn that," will spur you on to new successes.

- Don't be discouraged if you feel that other designers or members of your class seem to be producing better work than you—just concentrate on developing your own unique style.

- Allow yourself to learn. Don't worry if at first your work seems very influenced by the styles of others. It is through imitation that you will discover for yourself how to make the best use of the techniques.

- Don't worry if an experiment fails. A good designer is always pushing the boundaries. It is only through trial and error that truly original ideas will emerge. Congratulate yourself for having the nerve to go beyond the obvious, and ask what you have learned from the project.

- Don't be too fixed in your definition of "success," since this will close off avenues opened up by a happy accident. So long as you know what the rules are, it can be fun to break them sometimes.

- Use your instinct about what you have produced, and don't try to judge it through the eyes of others. Some people will love your work, others will hate it—all you can do is be true to your own take.

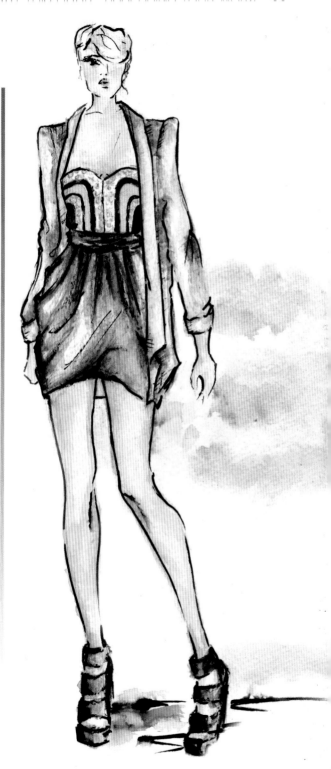

1 Finding inspiration

People often wonder how fashion designers manage to come up with so many marvelous new ideas. The truth is that these ideas are rarely completely new: designers create by reinventing the world around them. This chapter will show you how to develop designs from almost any inspirational source, whether you are exploring the world of fine art or the buildings of your town, Indian culture or the familiar objects in your home and garden.

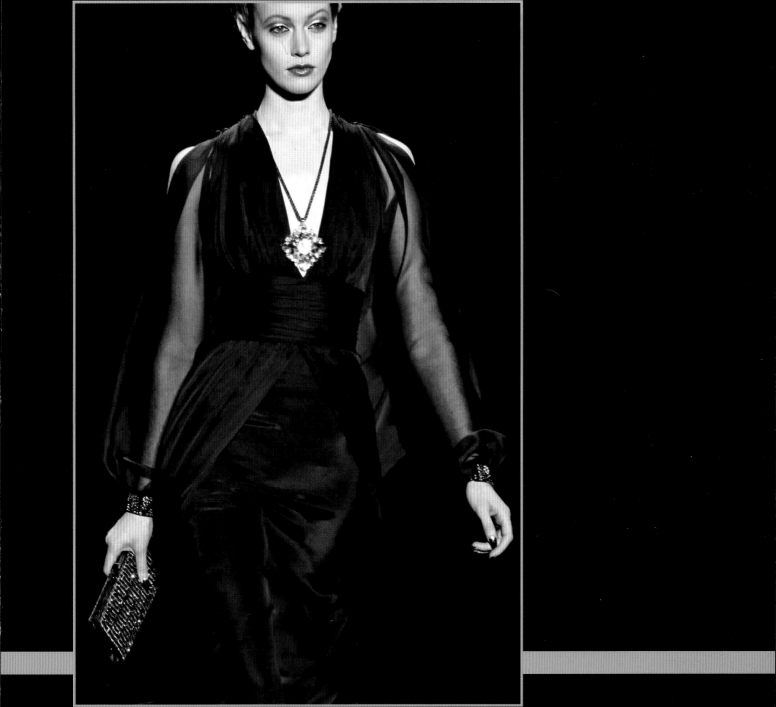

* Inspiration can come from music, movies, art, and the general zeitgeist of cultural events. An insightful designer will research all of these factors when designing.

* Mine the past: trends are often adapted from the past; the key is to give them a fresh feel.

Where to start

One of the most daunting aspects of creativity is being faced with a blank page, but luckily ideas don't have to be pulled out of thin air. A mistake often made by new fashion students is to design a series of individual garments that have no discernible source of inspiration and no cohesive "look." However, once you have established a theme, a multitude of related ideas will come tumbling onto your page.

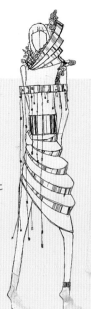

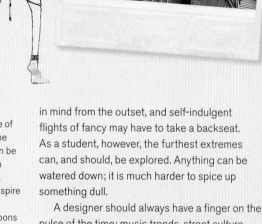

Inspiration for design themes can be found everywhere, whether your source is a seashell on a beach or a splendid skyscraper, the fun of the fair or the carnival at Rio. If you research well, your topic will automatically influence your garment ideas; for example, the theme of a circus or fairground is likely to produce a colorful, flamboyant look. With an inquiring mind, almost anything can trigger a creative spark. The trick is to be able to select the best route to follow. As a commercial designer, you will have your customer

▲ **LOOKING UP**
The angled elegance of structures such as the Chrysler Building can be captured in a fashion design. Why not let a multistory building inspire a tiered skirt, or add dangling beaded ribbons to mimic the pattern of its windows?

in mind from the outset, and self-indulgent flights of fancy may have to take a backseat. As a student, however, the furthest extremes can, and should, be explored. Anything can be watered down; it is much harder to spice up something dull.

A designer should always have a finger on the pulse of the time: music trends, street culture, movies, fine art movements. It is no coincidence that each fashion season has a discernible look; different designers often produce similar color ranges and silhouettes (the outline shapes of complete ensembles) because they are all aware of the broad trends. (However, designing from a completely off-the-wall angle has also produced some of fashion's greatest moments.)

Although nothing dates more quickly than fashion, looking to the past for inspiration often produces great results. A whole era can become an inspiration, and the popularity of different eras tends to wax and wane in cycles. One year styles from the 1950s might be in fashion; the next it's a '70s look that's popular. Designs that were the height of fashion become the object of derision, only to reemerge a generation later as "must have" articles; wide-flared, low-rise trousers are a perfect example.

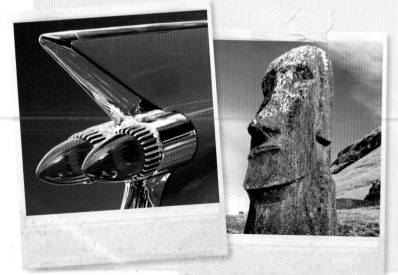

◀ **GLOBAL ICONS**
Give a design a 1950s feel by incorporating the distinctive shape of a Cadillac's tail fins (left). The Easter Island statues (right) are also iconic: references to these enigmatic figures in a fashion illustration could have a striking effect.

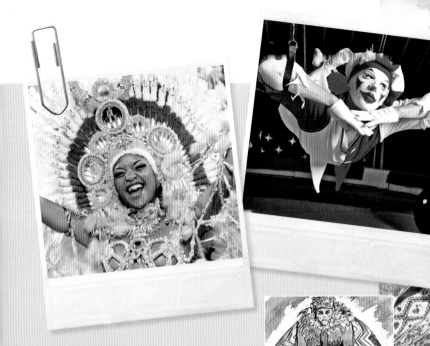

CHERRY-PICK IDEAS
Once you have thoroughly researched your source, you can choose the aspects that attract you most to include in your designs. You may decide to incorporate the complex color scheme, zigzag patterns, and layered look of clothes worn by Peruvian Quechua women; alternatively, it may be the trailing coat of a circus clown or a highly ornate carnival costume, reminiscent of tropical birds and flowers, that inspires you.

Structured sportswear has inspired many iconic shapes—think football shirts and Dynasty shoulder pads. Cycling Spandex produced a whole new fashion concept (skintight garments in bright colors), as did sailing wear, in the form of the synthetic waterproof clothing popularized by Tommy Hilfiger.

Patterns and styles based on ethnic ideas are recycled again and again by designers. One season they might work with the weaves of Latin American Indians; next year they might feature the prints of certain African tribes.

Fashion often draws on other forms of art for inspiration. The art deco magnificence, glistening reflections, and lofty symmetry of the Chrysler Building in New York make it a superb example of an artistic endeavor that could easily inspire garment design. Hollywood movies can also start fashion trends; *The Great Gatsby* and the *Mad Max* series popularized, respectively, 1920s flapper dresses and the "road warrior" look that combines punk and grunge.

Your opportunities for exploring themes are unlimited. You can research ideas by visiting museums or wandering through a city to draw and take photographs yourself, or you can absorb the paintings, sculptures, movies, photography, and books created by other people. The Internet is a great source of information that can be accessed from your home or college.

The knack of working with inspiration is to avoid trying to absorb too much at once. Being selective with your research and disciplined in developing just a few well-chosen themes will help you produce a focused range of designs that hold together as a collection.

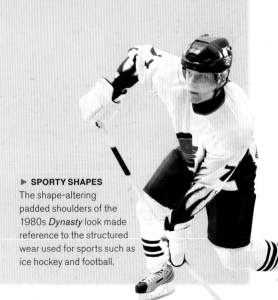

SPORTY SHAPES
The shape-altering padded shoulders of the 1980s *Dynasty* look made reference to the structured wear used for sports such as ice hockey and football.

UNIT 1 Drawing from your wardrobe

SELF-CRITIQUE
- Have you chosen the best clothes for the collection?
- Did you coordinate them well?
- Did you find the best medium to represent them?

It is never easy to put that first mark on a blank sheet of paper. A valuable exercise therefore is to practice drawing a collection consisting of garments that already exist. Coordinating these items and merchandising them in innovative ways can be a beneficial experience.

Considering the garment's function is crucial to the illustration. The purpose and season of an item should be coordinated with the style of illustration and the figure pose, to enhance the clothing's appeal.

Whatever approach you choose—casual chic, perhaps, or glamorous—the ideals of that approach should be represented. Explore how an overall image could be projected and better conveyed through the use of accessories and hairstyles, and make sure the illustration is bold. Be confident and work toward developing an individual style.

the project
Select three combinations of garments or outfits from your wardrobe, and look at current fashion magazines, or web sites, for trends and ideas you could incorporate. Make sure the garments can be combined effectively and be loosely described as a collection. Find a common theme that makes a cohesive visual presentation and unites all the pieces you select.

the objective
- Take a more detailed look at clothing that is familiar.
- Focus on different styling possibilities and color combinations.
- Think about how to best represent fabrics and present a cohesive image.

▲ CAPTURING THE COLOR
The garments selected here are all in primary colors, white, and black. This unites them and gives them a sense of being a collection.

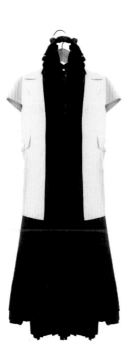

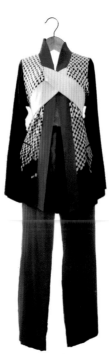

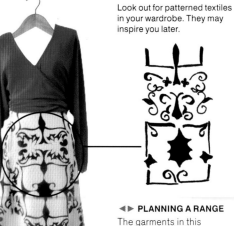

Look out for patterned textiles in your wardrobe. They may inspire you later.

◄► PLANNING A RANGE
The garments in this selection work well together because they are all tailored with soft, feminine details. The colors are primary and graphic, a fact that unifies the group. Make some quick sketches of the garments with pencil, ink, or markers.

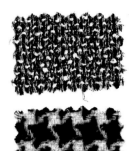

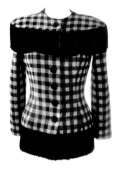

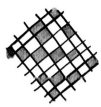

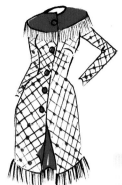

◄ CAPTURING THE TEXTURE
After creating these test drawings from the swatches (houndstooth and tweed), a variation on the fabric swatches can be rendered. For example, a red houndstooth and blue and yellow tweed could be created. These quick sketches make experimentation possible. You can then render different fabrics on the garments you have been drawing from your wardrobe.

the process
Hang the garments in front of you or print out photographs you take of them. Sketch some rough figures with your theme in mind. Create a color story with markers or colored pencils.

Next, try to give the collection an overall look. This can be achieved by unifying your theme through colors, silhouettes, accessories, and construction details.

Draw quickly to maintain a fresh, spontaneous feel to the work. Be bold and the sketches will remain fluid and animated. Continue making sketches until you are satisfied.

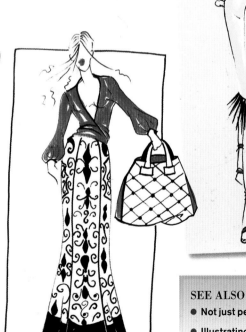

◄▼REMEMBER THE DETAILS
These practice sketches were made to explore trim ideas. The trims used here are: ruffles, beaded fringing, and contrasting ties.

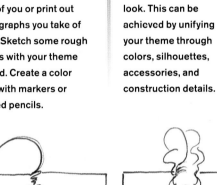

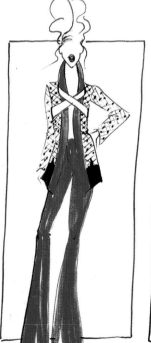

SEE ALSO
● Not just pencil, p. 80
● Illustrating bold print, p. 86
● Planning a range, p. 98

UNIT 2 Visiting a museum

Museums can sometimes seem dull or dumbed down to cater to schoolchildren. Don't be put off; a single collection of antiquities could keep a designer in ideas for a lifetime. Borrowing and adapting ideas from the past is not just acceptable in fashion design, but an essential way of obtaining raw materials. When you first visit a museum, it is best to spend at least half a day getting a general overview of the exhibits. Take the time to find objects that inspire you. It is only by looking more closely at a piece that its details and subtleties become clear, and only when you draw it can you be sure that you are truly observing it. Your sketchbook will then provide you with hundreds of starting points for planning a collection. Think both big and small: look at the overall shape of the object and also at the tiny detail. Play with scale, enlarging a detail and reducing the size of the piece as a whole. Don't restrict yourself to looking at historical clothes just because you are designing garments. Inspiration can come from ceramics, sculpture, jewelry, calligraphy, and even just from the ambience of the gallery.

You do not need to take along all your crayons and paints when you visit a museum. Make plenty of notes in your sketchbook so that you can develop your ideas when you are back at home or in the studio.

Exploring a source of inspiration through sketches and working drawings enables

the project

Visit a museum and browse until you find an area that inspires you. Make notes and observational sketches covering several interesting subjects. Then select a theme to inspire a small collection of garments that obviously reflects its source. Complete four finished design drawings at home or in your studio.

the objective

- Select a source that inspires you.
- Make judgments and choices before putting pencil to paper.
- Learn to observe an object carefully.
- Adapt designs from the past to create work that is uniquely yours.

the process

Research your local museum or visit a national collection. Spend at least half a day browsing before selecting what you want to concentrate on. Fill several pages of your sketchbook with color notes, doodles, and quick sketches of objects and details relating to an area that interests

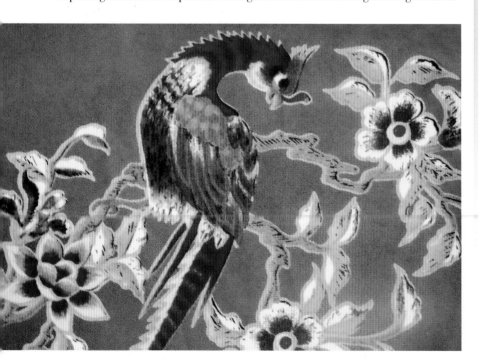

◀ **FASHIONS OF THE PAST**
Refer to historical pictures for intriguing images of garments, fabrics, and accessories worn in the past. The color palettes and shapes featured here can be used to inspire ideas for contemporary designs.

SEE ALSO
- Mood boards, p. 28
- Designing fabric ideas, p. 48
- Color palettes, p. 118

SELF-CRITIQUE
- Did you spend long enough selecting your source?
- Have you looked closely at its detail?
- Have you noted its overall look?
- Were your drawings useful to work from?
- Do your final drawings reflect the source?

you. Then choose a suitable source (a single object or small number of objects that you find inspirational) and make at least ten quick drawings on site of all its different aspects. Concentrate on the overall shape for some drawings and on minute details for others.

Back at home or in the studio, start working on your color palette (see page 118) and explore the possibilities of shape, exaggerating some of the lines, blocks, and planes in your drawings, and reducing others.

Consider how the aspects of the source that you have noted in your sketchbook—lines, colors, outline, mass, decoration, texture—might translate into fashion designs. Draw out some rough ideas for garments, and then add color. Finally, complete four finished design drawings.

▶▼ **BOLD REWORKING**
These working drawings show how sketches and notes made on site can be developed. Here, reference to fans, tattoos, jewelry, and Asian lettering all inspire modern creations.

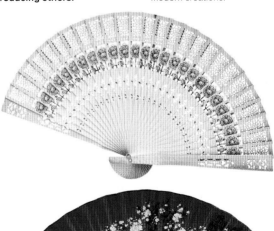

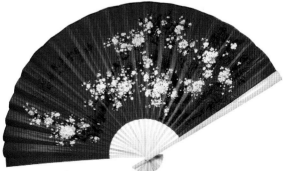

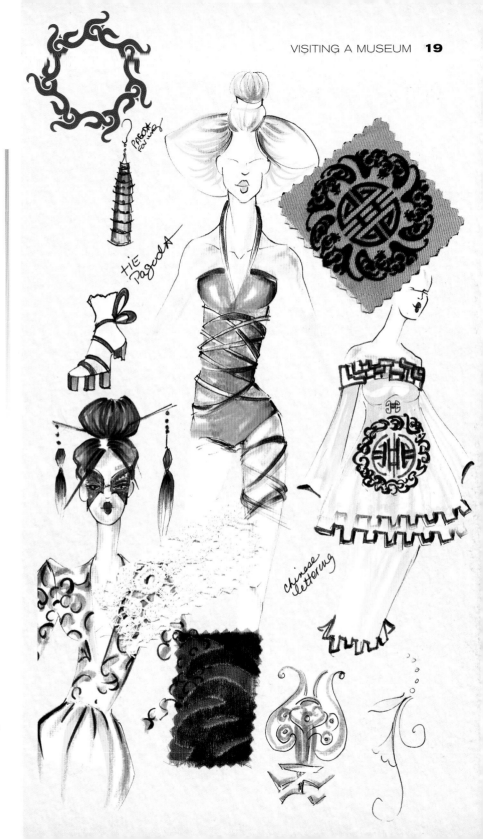

UNIT 2 Visiting a museum

fashion designers to target details they feel are important to a look or collection. Striking color combinations, elegant shapes, or an interesting detail in an old painting can all turn into a great garment concept. The illustrations featured here explore the theme of chinoiserie, reflecting the source's historical background and forming new designs based on this inspiration. The designs and sketches all echo the predominate features of the source. The influence of chinoiserie gives the sketches cohesion and sophistication.

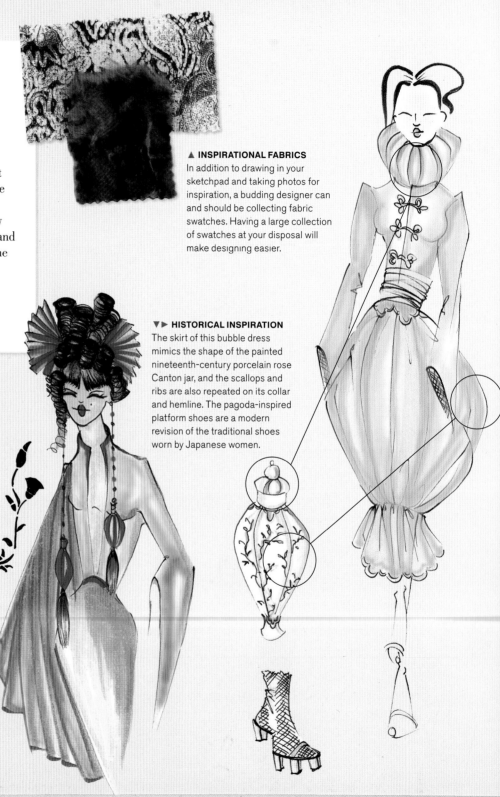

▲ INSPIRATIONAL FABRICS
In addition to drawing in your sketchpad and taking photos for inspiration, a budding designer can and should be collecting fabric swatches. Having a large collection of swatches at your disposal will make designing easier.

▼ ▶ HISTORICAL INSPIRATION
The skirt of this bubble dress mimics the shape of the painted nineteenth-century porcelain rose Canton jar, and the scallops and ribs are also repeated on its collar and hemline. The pagoda-inspired platform shoes are a modern revision of the traditional shoes worn by Japanese women.

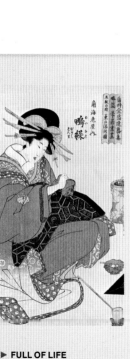

▶ FULL OF LIFE
Even when drawings are loose or abstract, they can still be comprehensive and telegraph a discernable trend or style. This fashion illustration draws on this Japanese image for its striking color palette.

▼ **OLD AND NEW**

The effect of these drawings is a vibrant mix of the historical and current. The work is fresh because the inspiration of chinoiserie has been brought into a modern context. These illustrations incorporate contemporary detailing such as hairstyles and accessories to create exciting styling.

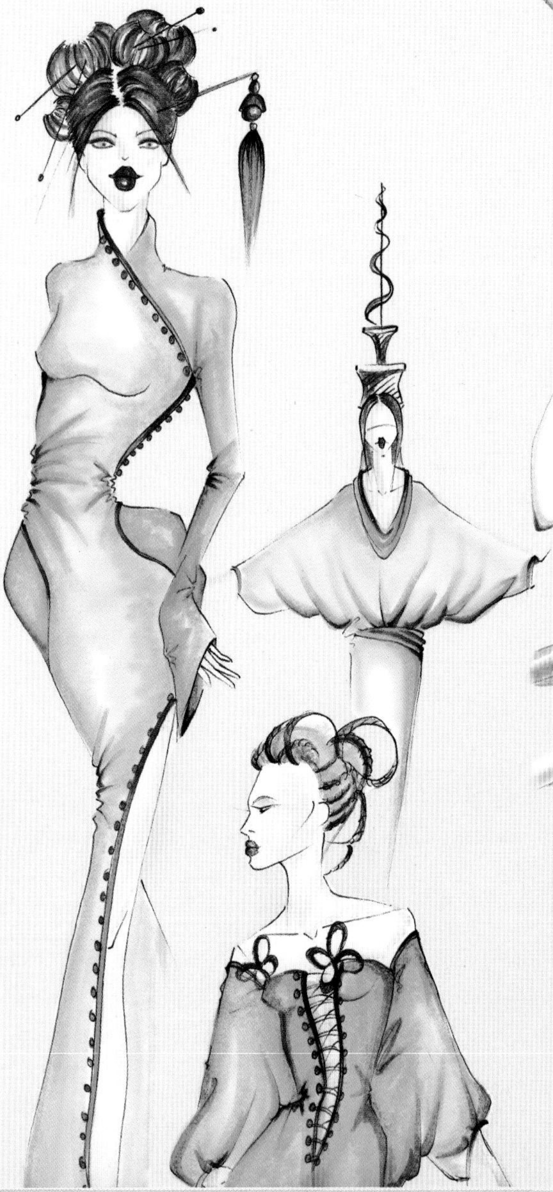

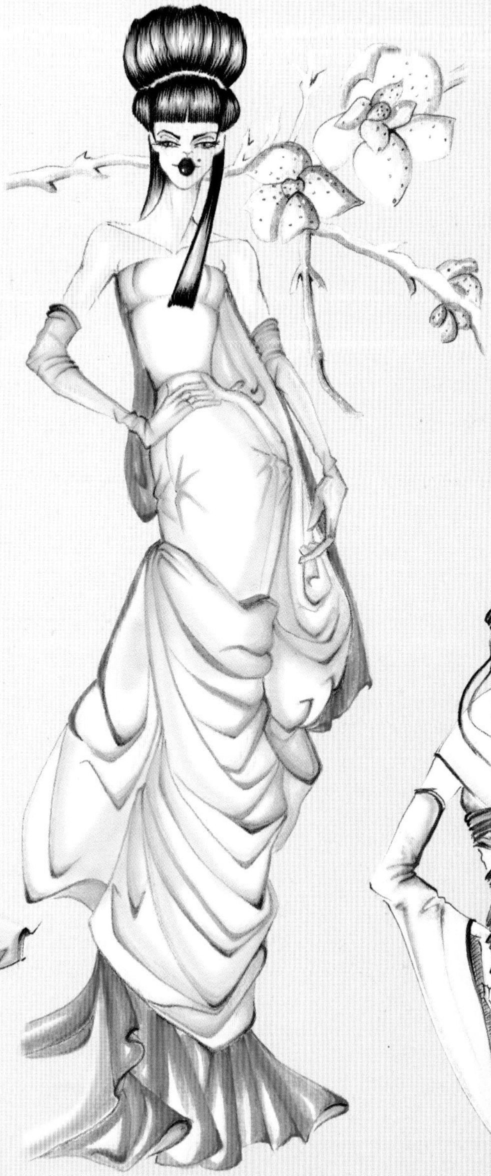

◀▼ **CONSISTENT COLOR**

The color palette of jade, rose, gold, and bronze is consistent in the group and based on research. This serves to increase the impression of a cohesive collection or group.

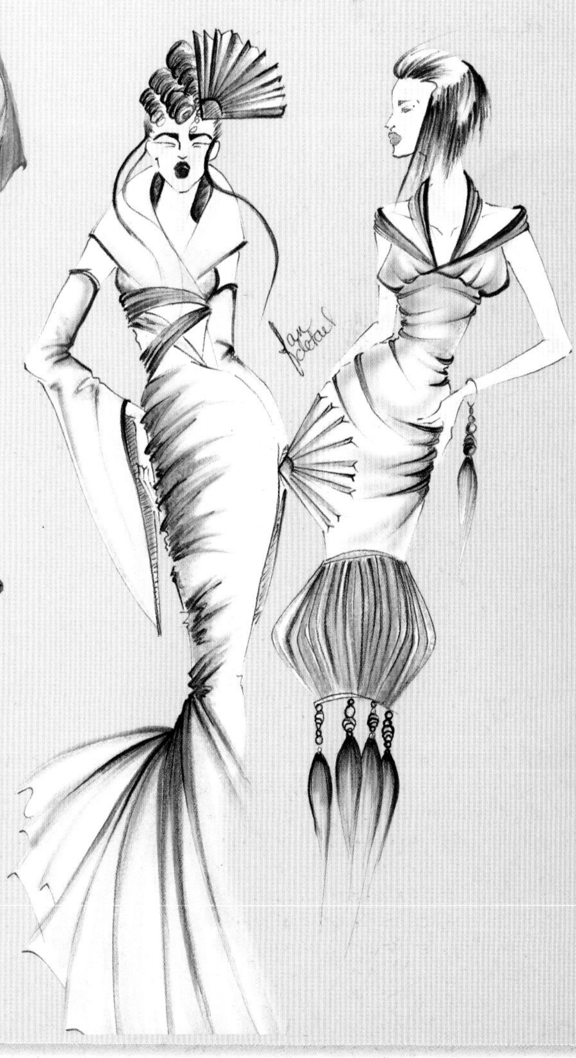

UNIT 3 Investigating architecture

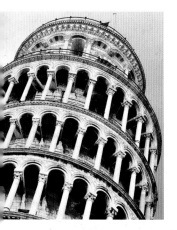

It may seem surprising to use buildings as inspiration for clothes. Building design is obviously meant for a long visual life, whereas fashion in clothes changes with each season. However, both forms are three-dimensional and structured, and whether it is in the overall theme of a building or just a detail, useful ideas are there to be found. If you set out to investigate architecture, you will discover a wealth of interesting textures, subtle colorways, and strong design features.

Whether you choose to study a historical building like a church, a famous modern landmark, or even your own home, ideas will emerge if you observe your source closely. The reflective glass of a skyscraper might suggest the use of a shimmering modern fabric; the peeling paint of an old beach hut could stimulate you to create a look incorporating ripped layers. The perspective lines of a building often provoke ideas about outline—the Guggenheim Museum could suggest a billowing blouse or the Chrysler Building might be incorporated into a tiered silhouette.

Whether it is the splayed lines of a railway station that inspire a sweeping pleated skirt or the curlicue

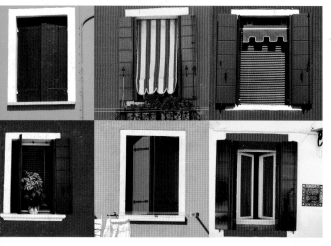

the project
Think in general about the sort of architecture that could spark some design ideas. Select a building and make extensive drawings in your sketchbook. Highlight the elements (such as overall shape, design details, and surroundings) that get you thinking. Take photographs. Then make photocopies of your research and work into them using paint, markers, and ink. Distill these ideas to illustrate four design ideas.

the objective
- Practice meticulously observing everything around you.
- Make judgments about the elements you want to use in your designs and those you reject.
- Use one form of creative work to create another.

the process
Start by looking through architectural magazines. Once you have decided what kind of architecture might inspire you, go out with a sketchbook and camera to select a building and record its shape and details. Look at stairwells, elevator shafts, windows, doors, decoration, colors, and textures, as well as at the overall shape. Record the building's

▲▶ **BOLD STATEMENTS**
The Leaning Tower of Pisa, some brightly colored windows, and the L'Hemisfèric building in the City of Arts and Sciences, Valencia, Spain, are all stunning examples of architecture that could inspire fashion design.

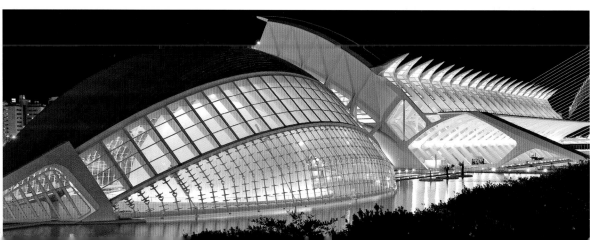

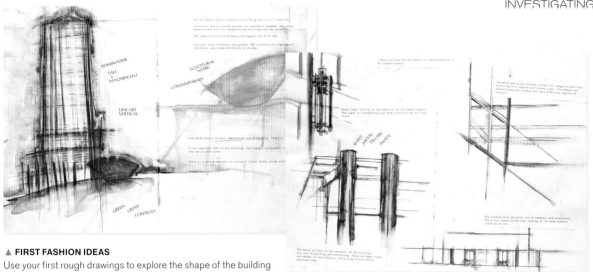

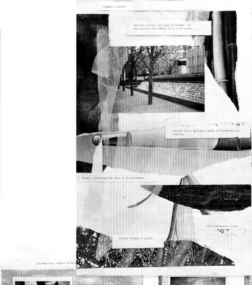

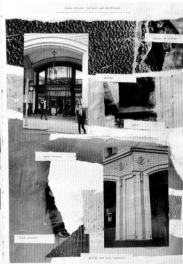

▲ FIRST FASHION IDEAS

Use your first rough drawings to explore the shape of the building as a whole. The fashion parallels, such as a long flared dress or skirt silhouette, will become apparent.

◀▼ DECONSTRUCTION

Consider the structure of the building in depth. Exploring the jointing details, for example, may inspire you to think about how the different parts of your garments will fit together. Try to match the colors and textures of your photographic research so that your fabric ideas reflect the source, too.

surroundings, too. Take photographs to capture the whole picture and make sketches to highlight the elements you want to remember. By making these choices, you will soon learn to discern what is of use to you and what to reject. Take photocopies of your photographs and sketches, which you can then work into with paint, markers, and ink, altering the image by manipulating certain elements to create something personal to you. Finally, combine these highlighted elements into four original fashion designs. It doesn't matter if the result is a million miles away from your starting point—the cables of a suspension bridge might have become cords supporting a silk bodice in your reworking of the concept—provided that the journey from source to conclusion is mapped out in your research.

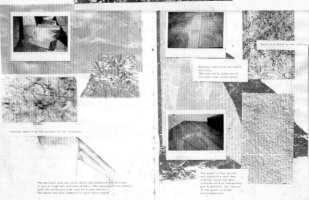

SELF-CRITIQUE

- Did you start with an interesting building?
- Did you make notes of the building's major themes and also of its details?
- Have you transformed one type of three-dimensional design into another?

SEE ALSO

- A fresh look at the familiar, p. 26
- Working drawings, p. 130

UNIT 3 Investigating architecture

work on a wrought-iron balcony that generates ideas about embroidery or ruffles, the inspiration for garment silhouettes and details can be found in almost any architectural source. When looking for fashion ideas in architecture, it is important to explore as many aspects of the starting point as possible. It may be an unexpected detail—such as, in this case, the arrangement of windows in a skyscraper—that becomes one of the salient features of the design. The illustrations featured here distill the gathered research into unique garment designs and move away from obvious references to the starting point while still retaining a sense of the original source.

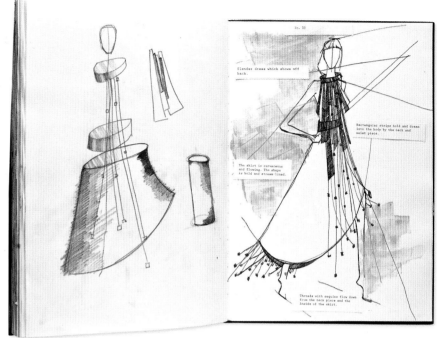

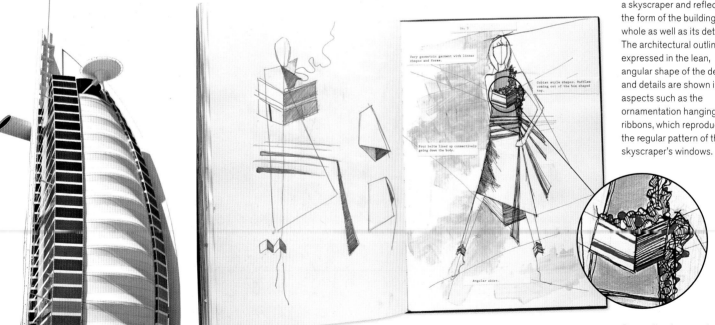

◀▲ **OUTLINE AND DETAIL**
These designs are based on a skyscraper and reflect both the form of the building as a whole as well as its details. The architectural outline is expressed in the lean, angular shape of the designs, and details are shown in aspects such as the ornamentation hanging on ribbons, which reproduces the regular pattern of the skyscraper's windows.

Decorative plasterwork or complex reflective patterns are a valuable source of inspiration for decorative finishing touches.

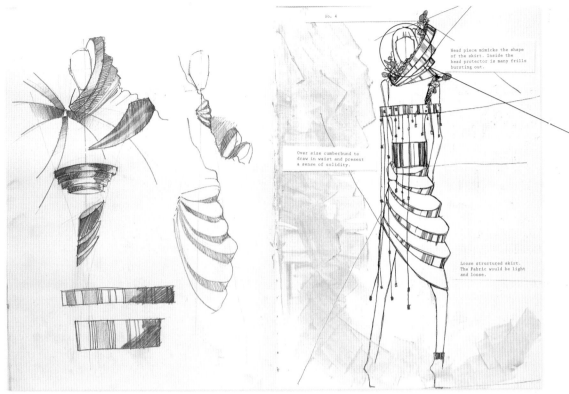

No. 4

Head piece mimicks the shape of the skirt. Inside the head protector is many frills bursting out.

Over size cumberbund to draw in waist and present a sense of solidity.

Loose structured skirt. The Fabric would be light and loose.

Architects and designers frequently have the same departure point of reference, so it is no surprise that one influences the other.

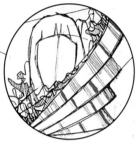

◀ **THE "GENES" OF THE IDEA**
These illustrations deconstruct the building, abstracting inspiring elements. In the process of developing a hard-edged design into the soft-edged format of a garment, the obvious references to the skyscraper have been lost. However, a strong sense of the parentage of the original source remains—the "genes" of the idea are still present, giving cohesion to the collection as a whole.

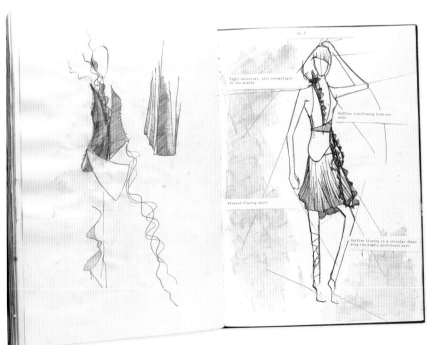

No. 5

Tight waistcoat, slit revealingly in the middle.

Ruffles overflowing from one side.

Floated flaring skirt

Ruffles flowing in a circular shape from the highly positioned hair.

▶ **USING MINIMAL COLOR**
The collection is given a unified feel by use of a dynamic illustration style and the effective use of minimal coloring. The understated palette of gray, black, and a hint of red reflects the original architectural source.

* Everyday objects
can provide a
unique source of
inspiration.

* The natural world
is full of great
shapes, patterns,
textures, and color
combinations.
Use them!

* Edit your
influences so that
you present a
coherent theme to
each collection.

A fresh look at the familiar

When discussing how fashion designers and illustrators work, people often wonder where all the ideas come from. How can a designer produce such a volume of original work each season, apparently out of thin air? The answer, of course, is that it does not just appear as if by magic but comes from the systematic development of ideas often triggered by the everyday world that surrounds us.

As a designer, you will learn how to look anew at commonplace objects and themes, and see in them possibilities for inspiration and creativity. Once this is understood, the mystery is exploded, and you can see how the world around you offers an endless source of imaginative potential.

This huge range of choice may appear somewhat daunting at first, but you will soon develop the ability to be selective with your starting points, based on their potential value to you as a source of inspiration. The key is to use images that truly interest and inspire you, and to investigate these concepts in an original way. An exciting personal approach to a concept will add a unique flavor to a design. With time, you may find yourself revisiting certain ideas and images. This is perfectly acceptable so long as you are able to find an original interpretation of your theme for each range of designs, and it is part of the natural development of your own recognizable design style.

As well as being of interest to you, it is important that your sources incorporate various factors that you will be able to use

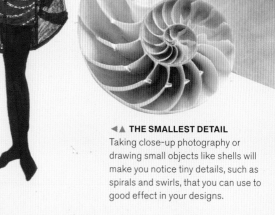

◀▲ THE SMALLEST DETAIL
Taking close-up photography or drawing small objects like shells will make you notice tiny details, such as spirals and swirls, that you can use to good effect in your designs.

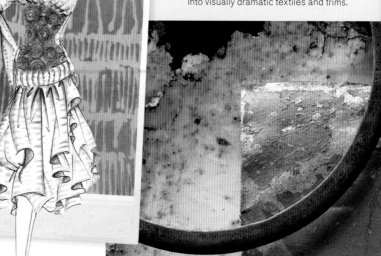

◀▼ THE NATURAL WORLD
Embroidery or lacework ideas can be derived from many different items in nature. A peacock's feather, a bamboo branch, a leaf, or undulating sandstorm lines all provide interesting textures and patterns. These natural patterns can be translated into visually dramatic textiles and trims.

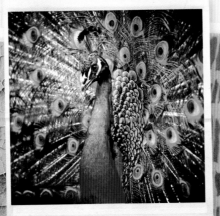

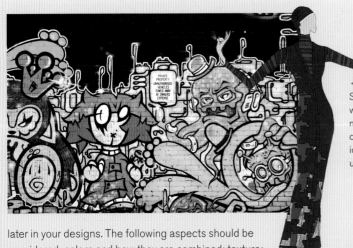

◀ POPULAR CULTURE
Street art makes a wonderful contrast to the natural world. Bright colors can inspire fantastic print ideas with a contemporary urban slant.

later in your designs. The following aspects should be considered: colors and how they are combined; texture; proportion; shape; volume; details; and decoration. Your starting point should satisfy your creative interest on as many of these levels as possible. You can then use your material to create mood boards (see page 28), which will provide a focus for the further development of selected aspects of your research and help you to be disciplined in designing garments based on a few well-chosen and targeted themes.

▶ THE TREASURES AT HOME
What interesting artifacts do you have stashed away at home? Look closely at an heirloom or a souvenir in order to appreciate it anew. Antique textiles, with their intricate patterns and rich tones, are a great source of inspiration and can be easily investigated through books, museums, and the Internet.

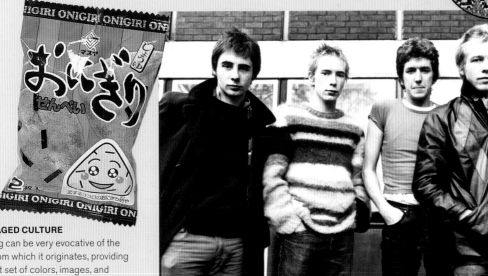

▲ PACKAGED CULTURE
Packaging can be very evocative of the culture from which it originates, providing a compact set of colors, images, and graphics that can convey the essence of an entire country.

◀ TAKE A CHANCE ON ME
Fashion runs in cycles; pop bands such as The Sex Pistols and the clothes associated with them are constantly going in and out of fashion. What "outdated" styles can be reinvented to create contemporary ideas?

UNIT 4 Mood boards

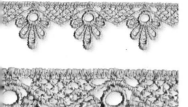

Creating a mood board is great fun and will help you to be selective with the research you have gathered. This is the first stage of organizing your thoughts and collected images, enabling you to channel your creative excitement toward a cohesive and targeted design outcome. Mood boards are made by arranging images and color ideas on a large board so that you can see at a glance how your designs might evolve. They vary in their complexity but, as the name suggests, mood boards should always capture the mood or flavor of your design project, as well as reflecting your target customer.

In grouping your researched images, you will have to make decisions about editing and prioritizing your selection, as well as confirming your season and color palette. Colors should reflect your chosen season— soft pastels will suggest a summer story, for example— but whatever the season, the color palette should be applied consistently throughout the project.

A successful mood board, like those pictured here,

SEE ALSO
● Creating a cohesive collection, p. 92
● Customer focus, p. 104
● Occasions, seasons, budgets, p. 108
● Color palettes, p. 118

▲▼ FABRIC SWATCHES
If you already have ideas about the fabrics that you will use for your final designs, include swatches on your mood board. Remember to keep the presentation clean, simple, and neat.

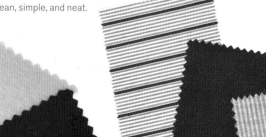

the project
Select a theme and season for your work, and consider who your target customer might be. Gather together all your research material. Using a 20- x 30-in. (50- x 75-cm) illustration board as a base, arrange and glue together the strongest images, and combine them with a color palette or fabric swatches to make a collage. Also include images from current fashion magazines that suit your chosen theme. Build a mood board that reflects the essence of your design project.

the objective
● Prioritize images from your collated research.
● Reflect your target customer and chosen season.
● Bring together creative inspiration and current fashion trends.
● Finalize a color palette.
● Create a mood board that summarizes your chosen design theme.

the process
Research a theme that inspires you, gathering items such as postcards, magazine images, and photographs. Selecting from this research will help you focus on what is important in the project. Combine this research with images and trend predictions from consumer and trade magazines, fashion web sites such as *www.style.com*, and top designers' web sites. Also gather images to reflect the season and your target customer (see pages 104 and 108).

Experience will teach you what size of board

SELF-CRITIQUE
● Have you created an easy reference tool to use when sketching your rough ideas?
● Have you reflected your season and target customer?
● Have you finalized your color palette?
● Have you used the most important images?
● Have you summarized your theme?

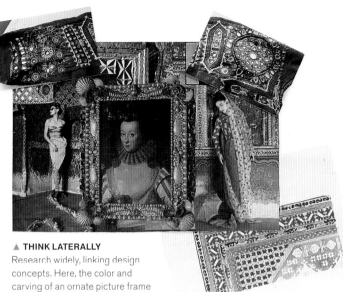

▲ THINK LATERALLY
Research widely, linking design concepts. Here, the color and carving of an ornate picture frame is visually married to intricately embroidered fabric and a luxurious sari.

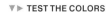
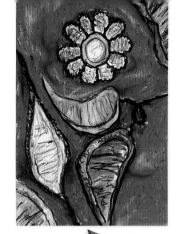

▼▶ TEST THE COLORS
Examine your chosen images together to identify the key shades and best color combinations to evoke your theme.

suits you best, but try starting with a 20- x 30-in. (50- x 75-cm) board that allows room for lots of images as well as swatches of yarns and fabrics, and any wording. Handwriting on a mood board usually looks unprofessional, so use lettering or a printout from a computer.

This is a good time to try putting together a color palette to include on your board, using paint swatches, color chips from Pantone books, or cuttings from magazines (for more information on working with color palettes, see page 118). Avoid including images that are not appropriate for your selected colors, because they will detract from the overall effect.

Ensure that all the images are cut out simply and stuck down neatly. It is the images that should grab the attention and not the manner in which you have mounted them. Simplest is always best.

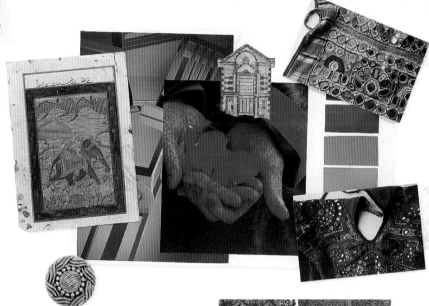

◀ MAGAZINE CUTTINGS
You should hoard a range of fashion magazines. Pick out current images that support your design ideas and include them on your mood board.

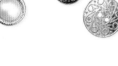

▲▶ REFINE YOUR CHOICE
Lay out all your gathered research material so that you can compare the images and select which to use on your mood board.

UNIT 4 Mood boards

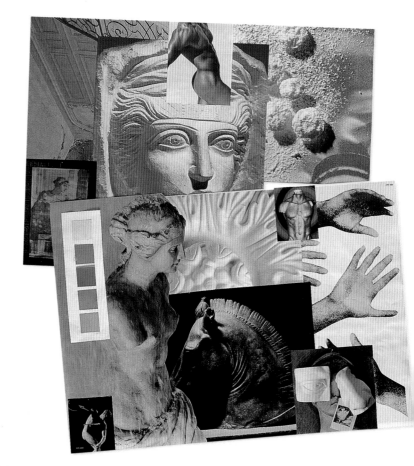

has a unique personality. It expresses the essence of the design ideas and sums up the theme, as well as reflecting practical concerns such as the season and the target customer. As the board is built up, combining inspirational items with pictures from magazines and information about upcoming styles, creative themes are married with current fashion trends. In this way, mood boards provide a focus for a creative yet commercial design solution.

The very act of deciding which images to include will help a designer narrow down and develop his or her ideas. As key ideas become prioritized, a clear thought process evolves, and the job of producing designs then becomes much simpler. The finished mood board should tell its own distinct story—being disciplined about creating only one board per project keeps creative efforts focused.

▲ **CLASSICAL INSPIRATION**
The classical theme of these boards has been inspired by textures and forms of sculpture. A muted color palette, derived from the colors of marble, helps to evoke a timeless and restrained mood.

◀ **SEASIDE NOSTALGIA**
This board combines the unlikely themes of the seaside and vintage dress (particularly dress associated with travel). The final collection was called "A '20s Trip to the Seaside."

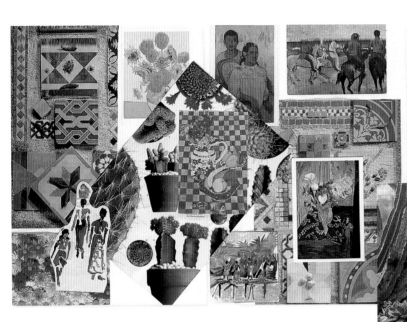

◄ **SUMMER COLORS**
A high-summer decorative theme has been created in this mood board through an eclectic mix of colorful images. This selection could be narrowed down further still to focus on artists, florals, or decorative tile work.

► **COHESIVE COLOR THEMING**
Images from fashion magazines can sit happily with research material. Here, folds of fabrics in shades of green create a common identity.

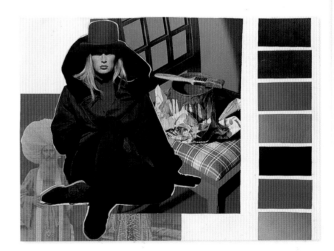

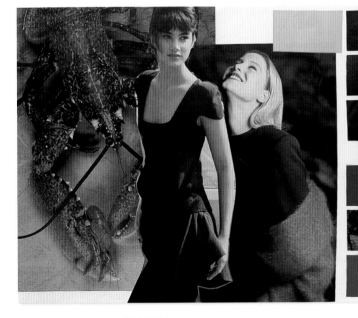

▲ **UNDERSTATED SOPHISTICATION**
Brown and neutral tones establish a sophisticated mood.

▲ **A FEMININE APPROACH**
This tonal palette of colors evokes a strongly feminine theme.

UNIT 4 Digital presentation boards

An effective and professional way to communicate your thoughts and to materialize your design ideas is to create presentation boards. There are a variety of such boards in the fashion industry depending on the end goal. A presentation board can be created to sell a product to buyers and investors, to communicate design concepts for a collection or season, or to forecast upcoming trends.

A presentation board can have a variety of visual elements. Most, however, can be categorized into three main areas: firstly, photos and pictures; secondly, fabrics and trims; and, thirdly, illustrations—including flats and draped/rendered figures. Depending on the type and purpose of the board, one or more of the above elements can be incorporated.

We look at two types of presentation board over the next six pages: digital mood boards and digital trend boards. A digital mood board is used to convey the feeling and emotional aspect of your design and to focus your thoughts on a given theme. A trend board is

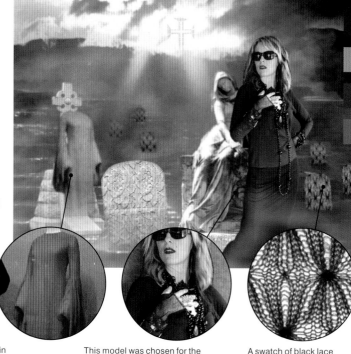

▶ **SOURCES**
In this composition, images of gothic tombstones and an atmospheric sky were selected and scanned into a computer along with digital photographs of fabric. All the material was opened and manipulated in Adobe Photoshop.

A photo of a mannequin wearing a medieval dress was scanned in, flipped left to right, and converted into gray scale for the final image.

This model was chosen for the central figure. Her skin and hair were placed onto a separate layer so that they could be altered to the desired colors without affecting the rest of the image.

A swatch of black lace fabric was physically scanned and imported into Photoshop to imitate the texture of tombstones.

the project
To create a digital mood board inspired by a unique decade.

the objective
- Find inspiration from the past.
- Use color as a tool to convey a certain mood.
- Create designs that capture the past yet are practical for today's fashion.
- Research and gather visual elements that can be used in a digital portfolio.

- Use Adobe Photoshop for the creation of a digital presentation board.

the process
Choose a popular movie of a past era (for example, a Brigitte Bardot movie of the 1960s) or a movie genre like, for example, gothic horror (see above). Pay attention to the garments, the accessories, the colors, the mood, and the overall style of the actors or characters. Next, look through the web and

various magazines in search of images and colors that capture the style and feel of the movie and its genre. Colors can have powerful effects on our feelings and can stir a variety of emotions, so take advantage of this fact by choosing a color palette that best conveys the desired mood. Illustrate three of your own designs inspired by the genre that are practical for today's fashion and complement them in your board. Gather all your materials and,

using Adobe Photoshop, create a mood board that best reflects the genre and its vibe. Here's how:
1 Keep all the photos, sketches, and materials you gathered organized in a folder on your computer.
2 Open a new file—a good size is 11 x 17 in. (28 x 43 cm) with a resolution of 150 dpi for web viewing. This will be your digital canvas or board.
3 Place your visual elements (fabrics, photos, illustrations)

roughly on your board. You can use Adobe Bridge to drag and drop desired files onto the board. In "Menu bar," go to File>Browse in Bridge.
4 Once you have your visual elements on the board, they will each be on a separate layer which you should name for ease of reference. You can then manipulate them individually to create the desired effect. Select the "Move" tool first, then in "Options bar" place a check mark next to

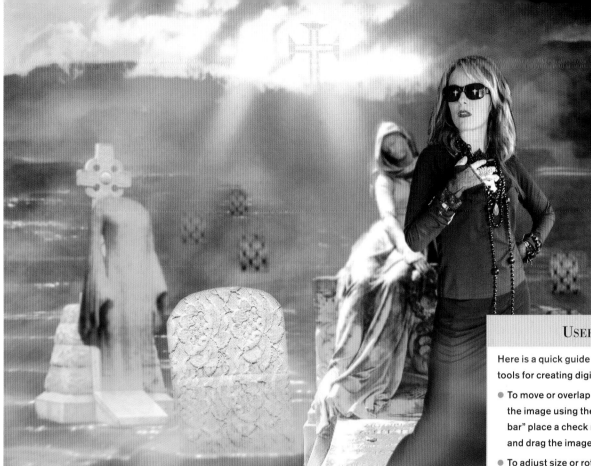

"Autoselect." Now every time you click on an image (click with the "Move" tool selected) on your board, that layer will be automatically selected for editing.

5 Now create a rough layout (the layout is the arrangement of the different elements of the board). Determine which orientation best suits your board (horizontal or vertical?) and rotate your canvas accordingly. In "Menu bar," go to Image>Image rotation.

6 Play with each of the layers and adjust their variables. There are many manipulations, including modifying image size, crops, color changes, opacity, overlapping layers, and using Photoshop filters.

SEE ALSO
● Mood boards, p. 28

▲ ADJUST TO EMPHASIZE

Notice how the blue adjustment increases the contrast to the red hair and creates a cooler, icy mood. Also, by softening the background the model appears sharper and becomes the focal point of the board. Having the face and hair of the model on a separate layer to the background will give you flexibility when it comes to coloring the cemetery.

SELF-CRITIQUE
● Are the digital files of a high-enough resolution to print (300 dpi)?
● Can you justify the colors used? Give reasons to use them for mood or market.

USEFUL TOOLS

Here is a quick guide to some of the most useful tools for creating digital presentation boards.

● To move or overlap an image on another, select the image using the "Move" tool, in "Option bar" place a check mark next to "Autoselect," and drag the image around the board.

● To adjust size or rotate an image, go to Edit>Free transform.

● To crop an image (be careful not to crop the entire board), use the "Rectangular marquee" or "Lasso" tool to select unwanted areas, and enter "delete" on the keyboard.

● To adjust the color, go to "Menu bar," then Image> Adjustment> Color balance.

● To change the opacity of an image, select its layer and, in the "Layers" palette, adjust the opacity to below 100%.

● To create dimension, add a drop shadow to your image. In the "Layers" palette, double click the desired layer (click away from its name). When the "Layer style" panel opens, under "Blending options," place a check mark next to "Drop shadow."

● To write text, select the "Type" tool from the toolbox, then drag and create an adjustable area for the written text.

UNIT 4 Digital presentation boards

used to provide designers with inspiration, ideas, and color palettes as well as resources about fiber and fabric technologies. Trend boards are a more targeted device used to telegraph specific silhouettes, colors, textures, construction details, and styling nuances. Mood boards are conceptual and generally convey a mood, while trend boards are more factual and definitive, explaining tangible details.

A digital mood board is simply a mood board in digital format. The digital version can be E-mailed, presented in PowerPoint or PDF format, and quickly changed if need be. Digital media offers the ability to immediately deliver the mood board to the client. In today's fast-paced marketing environment, a client wants to see the results as soon as possible, and as a designer there is immediate gratification in being able to make changes and updates quickly. Another advantage of a digital mood board is that it is more portable, because you could carry dozens of digital boards in your pocket on a USB drive.

Trends are not newly conjured up to sell clothing, but are dormant until creative minds dig them up.

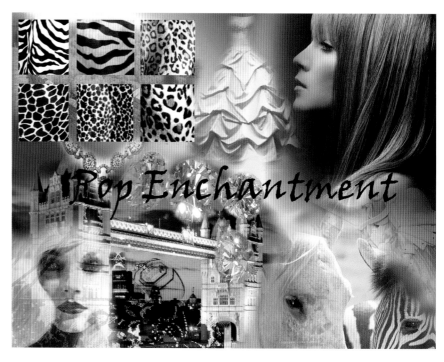

▲ BLENDING OF COLOR AND LIGHT
Digital software can create blending and color matching effects that allow for quick fabric color changes. In this mood board, multiple images were placed on different layers in Photoshop in order to utilize the "Layers blend" mode. This mode allows layers to interact with each other. Interesting transitions of color and light can then be created.

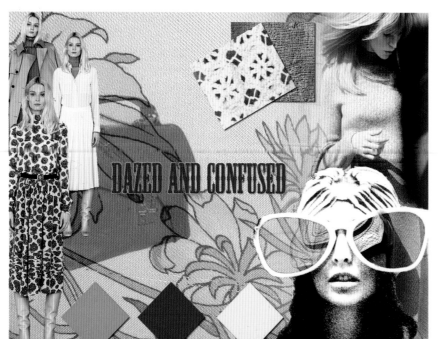

◀ MATCHING COLOR AND FABRIC
These images were created using the "Hue saturation" tool in Photoshop. Adjusting fabric color in order to match a photograph and convey a trend is one of many useful techniques available to the Photoshop user. This tool can reduce or change colors in any fabric to match swatches or photographs. Images can then be placed on different layers, like a deck of cards, shuffled, then stacked according to preference.

These creative minds have keen eyes for detail or hooks that will capture the attention of the buying public. Designers, stylists, insiders, futurist trend spotters, merchandisers, and those who offer predictive services are faced with the task of how to best understand and present new trends every season.

A digital trend board should showcase the trend and show the digital skill of the designer. Its advantage over a traditional one is the ability to quickly make changes to the color, layout, scale, and output of the images.

These trend boards include an interesting selection of images and illustrate adjustments that can be made with Photoshop, such as eliminating the old background when placed on the new board and making changes to color and lighting. The background photographs allow designers to express the overall concepts that the garments are meant to evoke.

Trend and forecasting services gather resources and information; they provide them in organized and visually appealing formats (printed and digital presentation books) for designers and companies to use. They collect images and stories of what's going on in fashion around the globe to predict color and trend direction, and to provide inspiration for runway shows,

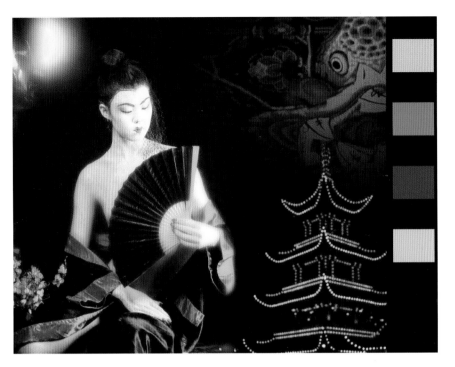

△ INSPIRATIONAL MOODS CREATED WITH IMAGES
Painting with images and adjusting opacity as images overlap can only be done in a digital environment. The original colors in this image were red (fabric, dragon, lipstick, pagoda, and flowers). By adding a "Hue and saturation adjustment" layer, the colors were "painted" in. This process created the blue-and-green color story.

▶ INFLUENCES OF THE PAST WITH TODAY'S TECHNOLOGY
For this mood board, the color scheme was selected first, then the images and fabric where chosen. Fabric can be changed to match the desired colors by using the "Image adjustment" color index. Selecting the image adjustment color table tool will show the amount of colors in the swatch. You can then control or select each color and match, change, or manipulate that color.

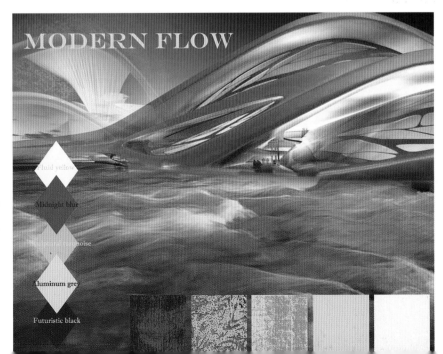

MODERN FLOW

Fluid yellow

Midnight blue

Sculptura turquoise

Aluminum grey

Futuristic black

UNIT 4 Digital presentation boards

trade shows, up-to-date retail store window visuals, and flats and illustrations. You can create your own trend board based on your research and inspiration. Some popular forecasting services are: Here and There (Doneger group), WGSN, and Trend Union (Edelkoort Inc.).

Traditional or digital?

Take a moment to compare how you would go about creating a traditional presentation board versus a digital board. Using a digital mood board as an example, you can gather (either electronically or by scanning) desired photos and fabrics that relate to your theme, then vary their sizes, color, opacity, and location with much more ease than the traditional cutting and pasting techniques. Another advantage is that the same elements can be reused for other boards and projects. For example, the same piece of fabric can be used for multiple boards. Once you work on your digital board, you'll realize that the design possibilities are endless.

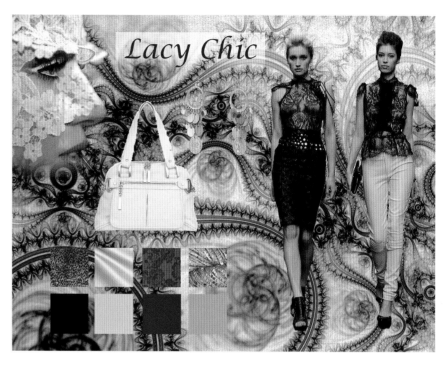

▲ **FOCUS**
In the "Lacy Chic" trend board, the focus is on feminine silhouettes and fabric, combined with tailored details. This unexpected combination is a fresh approach to using traditional lace fabric. Jean Paul Gaultier frequently references this masculine/feminine paradox and sees it as a modern approach to dressing. The colors used here are consistent with this trend.

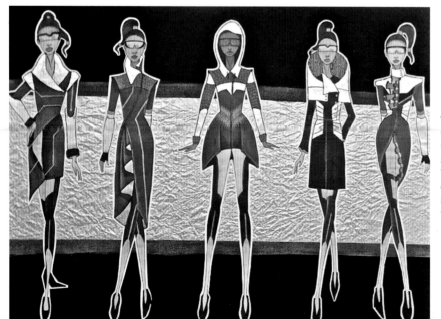

◄ **CONTINUITY**
When creating trend boards, continuity of color and theme can tie a collection or group together. This "urban" collection was a pencil and pen drawing that was colored digitally. The trend board aims to convey a biker-chic look, expressed with dark, reflective fabrics. The figures' sunglasses create a continuous theme that implies they are all from the same world.

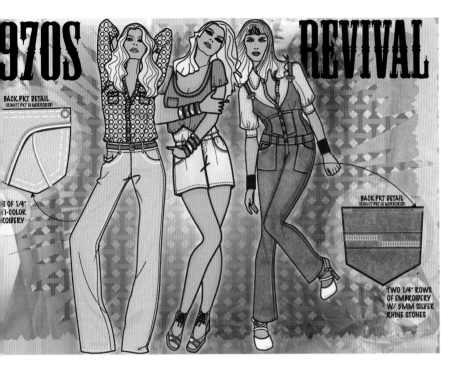

Planning your digital board

Planning is essential in creating a professional board. The first step in planning is to define the "purpose" of your presentation board. Is it being used to communicate fabric ideas? Is it aimed at forecasting a trend? The next step is to have a focus; here you should know your market (who is your customer?) and what your product is (what are you designing?). Once you've done this, gather all your visual elements so that you can begin roughly arranging your board's components to determine the best layout, orientation, and the total number of boards you need.

▲ **DIGITALLY MODIFIED FABRIC**
The collection in this board was inspired by 1970s fashion, but the garments have been updated to make them more suitable for women today. Garments like the '70s-inspired collared shirt print and the dungaree denim stitchwork have been rendered with digitally modified fabrics. Details of the pocket designs are enlarged to show off the digital stitchwork.

▶ **BACKGROUND DESIGN**
Each board has a background composed of separate images on separate layers so that they can be manipulated individually. The layers should be blended and their opacity lowered so as not to distract from the figures in the foreground.

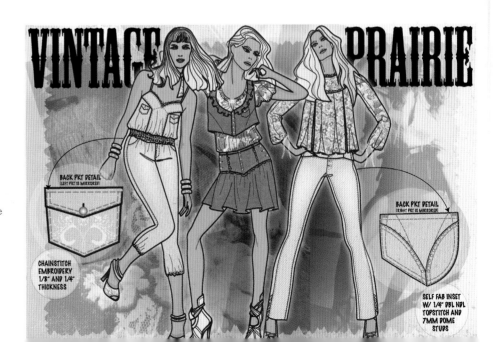

UNIT 5   The traditions of India

In this age of global branding, it can be refreshing to turn to non-Western cultures in search of inspiration. India is a great example of a culture that preserves a strong identity in the modern world because it is still very much connected to its traditional roots. The wonderfully vibrant colors and intricate shapes of India are a marvelous source of design ideas, whether drawn from the brilliant shades of the spices and printed fabrics, or ornate gold jewelry, or cloth woven with tiny mirrors, or the patterns of henna hand tattoos. These colors and shapes have been part of Indian culture for centuries and continue to be preserved by Indian communities around the world, so you should have no problem gathering your research.

By drawing on a source that is strongly traditional, you ensure that your materials never date—because they are not subject to the whims of fashion. As a design student you should explore as many cultures as possible; you will uncover a treasure trove of designs that with only minor adjustments of scale or color can produce completely fresh ideas.

This project is a great opportunity to express yourself—so be as flamboyant as you like! Later in the course you will be

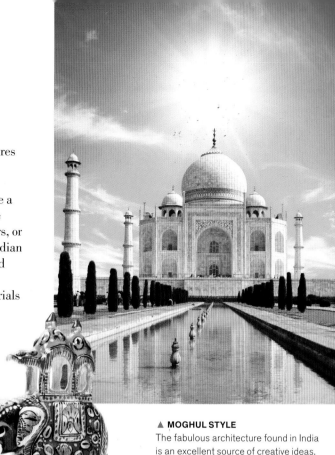

▲ MOGHUL STYLE
The fabulous architecture found in India is an excellent source of creative ideas. The dome of the Taj Mahal might suggest the full curve of a bodice, while the intricate inlay that covers its marble walls would create a stunning effect traced in silver thread on an evening gown.

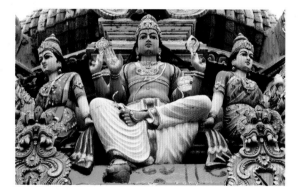

▲ LEGENDS OF THE GODS
In India, you are never far from the Hindu gods and goddesses, whose stories are depicted everywhere—on posters and cards and in countless movies and songs. You may be inspired by the gaudy colors, the kohl-darkened eyes, or the ancient dress of these typically Indian images.

SEE ALSO
● A fresh look at the familiar, p. 26
● Working drawings, p. 130

the project
Research Indian culture from as many sources as possible. Gather Indian items, find fabric swatches, take photographs, and make drawings and collages. Fill twenty pages of your sketchbook with all sorts of gathered research as well as your own work. Then start working into these found items, exploring the colors and shapes you might want to use in your designs. Restrict yourself to four finalized design drawings.

the objective
● Research Indian culture to draw on the design ideas of a non-Western culture.
● Put an original spin on these ideas.
● Achieve an interesting mix of cultural influences in your work.

the process
Research Indian culture by visiting museums, libraries, specialist food stores, markets, and temples. Buy postcards, take photographs, and make written as well as sketched notes while you are researching. Look for mirrored bags, spice samples, religious icons, and makeup designs. Listen to Indian music and watch Indian movies.

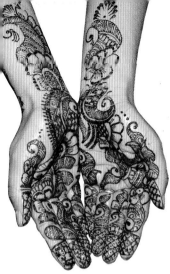

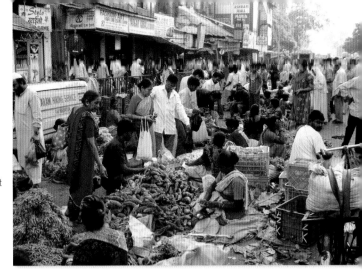

◄ VIBRANT COLORS
Delicate gold jewelry or the intricate patterns of henna hand-painting can be translated into textile design, perhaps using printing, embroidery, or beading.

► STREET LIFE
Heaps of fresh produce for sale in a street market may inspire you to try to match the glowing tones of eggplant, or perhaps to incorporate the shape of a coriander leaf into your designs.

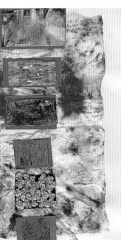

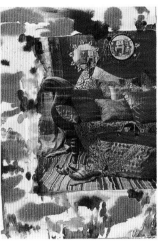

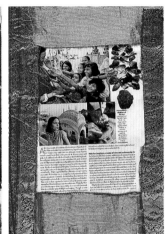

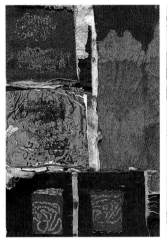

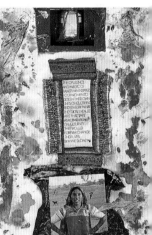

Immerse yourself totally in the research, and fill your sketchbook with cuttings, samples, swatches, and any style directions you may wish to follow.

Once you have some ideas, start working into your research, first highlighting and then manipulating the inspiring elements with paint, crayon, and ink. Try to match colors by mixing paints to achieve the perfect tone. This is harder than you might imagine, so experiment with color combinations. Try different effects, using chalk, transparent paint washes, or crayons applied lightly over dried paint, to achieve the color and texture of your source material. (When matching colors, you may also find it helpful to refer to the numbered Pantone color chips. See page 118 for more details.)

Finally, complete four fashion drawings inspired by your research. Try to give them an overall look, perhaps through a uniform color scheme or silhouette theme.

▲ FILL YOUR SCRAPBOOK
Organize your research by making your sketchbook into a scrapbook and filling it with as much colorful, stimulating material as you can. Gather photographs, textual information, fabric samples, images from magazines, and any other design references that inspire you, such as examples of Indian scripts. As you arrange your research, you will begin to assemble a mood concept and formulate a color palette.

SELF-CRITIQUE
● How well have you researched Indian culture?
● Have you matched the colors and textures from your research?
● Do your finished drawings give a new perspective on the source or are they just derivative?

UNIT 5 The traditions of India

considering issues such as customer profile and budget, so now is the time to explore some wilder flights of design fancy.

Designs inspired by traditional Indian dress might be loose and flowing, or involve the clever use of wrapping and layering as seen in turbans and saris. The color scheme may well be boldly vibrant, reflecting the rich tones of the source material. When exploring an ethnic source, it is important to gather as many cultural references as possible so that the sketchbook research and mood inspiration gels into work that retains the distinctive feel of the subject matter without being derivative. Traditional, non-Western cultures offer the designer a wonderful source of fabric, silhouette, and embellishment ideas. However, a successful design will always put a new spin on these traditional ideas, perhaps melding them in an original way or incorporating contemporary influences to create an original concept out of an ancient design. The collection pictured here strongly reflects its cultural starting point while remaining essentially multicultural in feel.

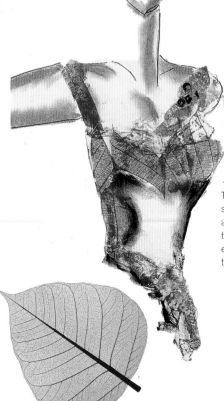

◀ **EMBELLISHMENT**
The use of found items such as leaves, flowers, and beads collaged onto the images gives an evocative textured feel to these illustrations.

◀▲▶ **FUSION FASHION**
This striking collection takes the textures and colors of India into a new context, transforming the original theme into another concept altogether. The rich, patterned fabrics and swirling skirts clearly reflect the Indian source, and the Western-style low-cut bodice contributes to the modern feel of the design.

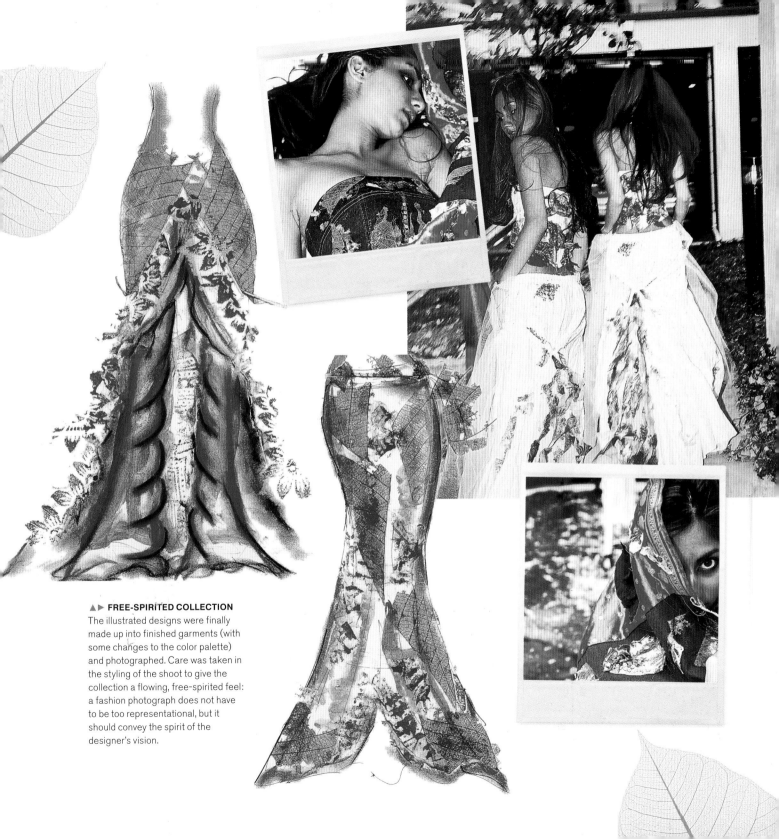

▲▶ FREE-SPIRITED COLLECTION
The illustrated designs were finally
made up into finished garments (with
some changes to the color palette)
and photographed. Care was taken in
the styling of the shoot to give the
collection a flowing, free-spirited feel:
a fashion photograph does not have
to be too representational, but it
should convey the spirit of the
designer's vision.

UNIT 6   Fine art and graphics

An important area for the fashion student to explore is print design, and one of the best sources of inspiration for this is the world of fine art. A print designer should be able to imitate the structure and style of a painting, and keep true to its color palette. Twentieth-century modernist painting provides especially rich material, since the fresh brushwork and bright colors lend themselves very well to print designs. Painters favored by textile designers include Dufy (who was himself also a print designer), Mondrian, Kandinsky, Miró, Matisse, and Picasso.

An alternative source is public domain graphic material. This is easily accessible as, for example, books or as clip-art images, available free through the Internet. Great results can be achieved by adapting and coloring these illustrations.

There are no rules about which motifs can be best repeated—in fashion print anything goes! However, if designing a print for a specific garment, you need to consider the cut of the fabric. Prints follow the fabric's grain, so cutting fabric on the bias (diagonally to the grain) will reorient the print. A "one-way" print, where motifs are aligned in one direction, has less cutting flexibility than an "all-ways" print.

The lines, shapes, and patterns of existing works of art and graphics can provide great inspiration for

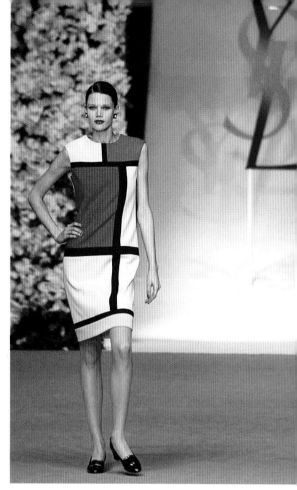

▶ CREATING ART FROM ART
The strong shapes and colors in the work of painters such as Mondrian lend themselves very readily to print design. Here, key aspects of the original painting were abstracted to achieve a design that refers recognizably to its source yet is itself a unique and beautiful creation.

▼ SALABLE DESIGNS
"All-ways" prints are usually more salable than "one-way" designs (which are less economical to use for garments, because more fabric is required to align the print correctly).

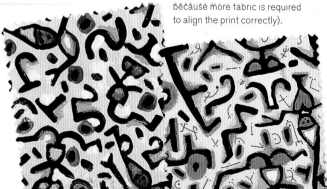

the project

Choose either fine art or graphic material as your source. For the first approach, try to imitate the style of a painting that you like and design five textile print patterns. For the second, rework your source material by photocopying, enlarging, and adding marks to create a square design for a headscarf. Try at least three colorways (i.e., make three versions of the design in different combinations of colors).

the objective

- Observe in detail the source material, noting colors, brushstrokes, and textures.
- Experiment with scale and coordination.
- If you choose the scarf option, discover how a change of colorway can alter the dynamic of a design.

the process

If you decide to design the print patterns, research some postcards of paintings that you think

may be suitable to convert into a repeatable print idea. Choose one picture, and observe its various sections and details. Then design at least five prints. Try to work in the style of the artist, taking care to use the same density of color and similar handling of paint or crayon. It can be interesting to experiment with different scales of shape and also to make two or more designs coordinate (because the designs come from the same source, there is a

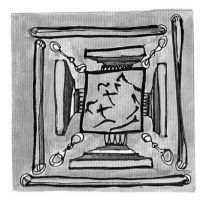
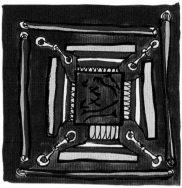
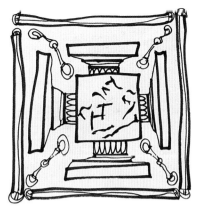

◄ BUILDING A DESIGN
These illustrations demonstrate a progression from graphic material to rough print design. The motifs were selected and sketches were made to test the design and the color scheme. The motifs were then arranged in the chosen design, which was photocopied to allow for the use of different colorways.

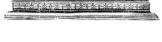
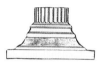

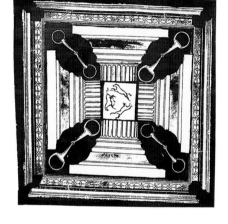

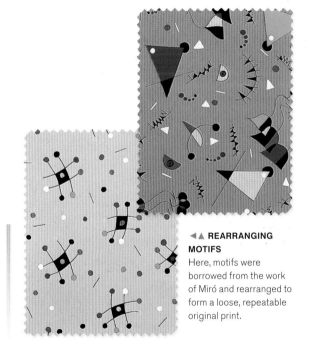

◄▲ REARRANGING MOTIFS
Here, motifs were borrowed from the work of Miró and rearranged to form a loose, repeatable original print.

good chance that they will coordinate automatically). Try designing both "one-way" and "all-ways" prints. You will be pleasantly surprised at how many great print ideas can come from just one painting. For the scarf project, select your graphics and make creative use of a photocopier. You can blow images right up so that the edges begin to fragment, giving an interesting texture. Then cut out shapes and arrange them in several ways, differing

the scale. These images can be juxtaposed with fine lines or other markings. Also experiment with color combinations. When you are satisfied, commit yourself to a design. Stick down the black-and-white images, and photocopy them several times to work on your chosen colorways. You can then work into the designs with paint, crayon, and ink. It is often best not to use too many colors; by restricting yourself, you simplify the process of

balancing colors. You will see that making different colorways of the same design can achieve very diverse results.

SELF-CRITIQUE
● Could you imitate the style of your chosen painter?
● Did you make the painting or graphic your own by using it in an unexpected way?
● Did you experiment with scale and coordination?
● Are your colorways balanced?

SEE ALSO
● Investigating architecture, p. 22
● Illustrating bold print, p. 86

UNIT 6 Fine art and graphics

fashion designers. There isn't a painting in the world that couldn't be made to yield ten print designs, and the potential for manipulating graphic material is endless. The key to success in the first part of the project—using fine art to create print design—is to observe the works in great detail and imitate closely the style and techniques of the painter. In their bold geometric lines, the print patterns shown here have a clearly recognizable source in paintings by Dufy and Mondrian, while being at the same time original designs.

The different colorways of the scarf designs demonstrate how dramatically a new color palette changes the look of a piece. It is often best not to use too many colors; restricting the color palette simplifies the process of balancing colors and makes it easier to achieve a strong statement.

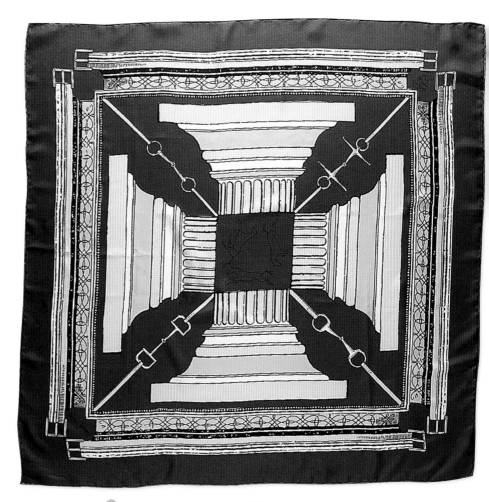

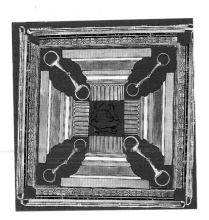

▲ **DIFFERENT COLORWAYS**
The scarf prints were made in different combinations of colors, demonstrating how much a simple alteration in coloring can change the look of a design.

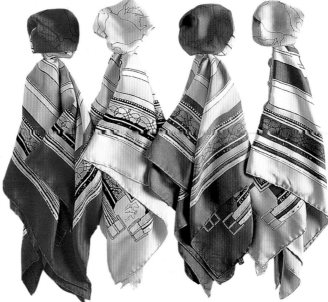

◄▲ **AN INTEGRATED DESIGN**
The final scarf print has been slightly altered in minor details but still reflects clearly its journey from individual graphic motifs to integrated design. The individual components have been blown up or reduced in scale, using a photocopier, to produce an interesting divergence in line strength.

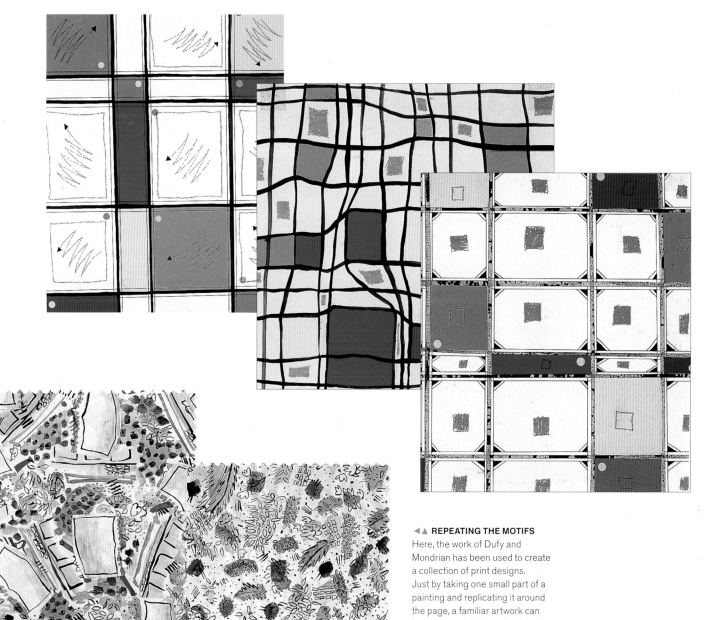

◄▲ **REPEATING THE MOTIFS**
Here, the work of Dufy and
Mondrian has been used to create
a collection of print designs.
Just by taking one small part of a
painting and replicating it around
the page, a familiar artwork can
be reinterpreted into a fresh and
striking print design.

Small details, big ideas

* Put a new spin on a familiar concept by exaggerating fine details.

* Look closely at an everyday object for an interesting color palette and surface detail.

* Reference books on unrelated topics, such as science, can bring new ideas.

One simple way to see something in a fresh light is to experiment with its scale. If a small part of a commonplace object is blown up to a much larger scale, it will appear new, and instead of being boring and familiar might become the source of creative ideas. It is this sort of in-depth consideration of a source that puts an individual stamp on your work.

By describing the details of an image or object in a much larger scale—through drawing, photography, embroidery, or using a photocopier—you will have already started the creative process. When experimenting with scale in this way, it is useful to try to abstract the elements that most interest you, instead of aiming simply to create a realistic representation of your topic. For example, a close-up of insect wings may inspire you to create some original color combinations or scalelike patterns. Let your series of drawings or photographs evolve to become increasingly abstract. This process of selection and development is important—you are on your way to creating a unique design solution inspired by your research. Ask yourself why you are attracted to the images you have chosen: what is it about pebbles or snowflakes that interests you? The answer will point your developments in the right direction; this is what you should try to capture as you abstract out the important elements of your research. In this way, something as ordinary as paint peeling from a wall will become a wonderful mine of ideas for layers of texture and color—and you will start to see that wall through the eyes of a designer.

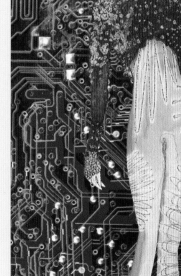

▶ **INSPIRATION UNDERFOOT**
Pebbles could be investigated individually, in terms of their subtle texture and flecks of contrasting colors, or could be seen as a group of similarly shaped objects that could generate a random print pattern.

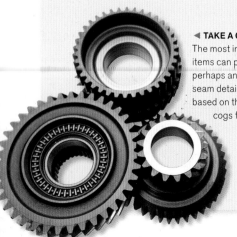

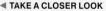
◀ **TAKE A CLOSER LOOK**
The most insignificant items can provoke ideas—perhaps an interesting seam detail could be based on the way these cogs fit together.

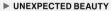
▶ **UNEXPECTED BEAUTY**
Some man-made objects are extremely beautiful when seen up close. This circuit board might inspire ideas for beading or textured knitwear.

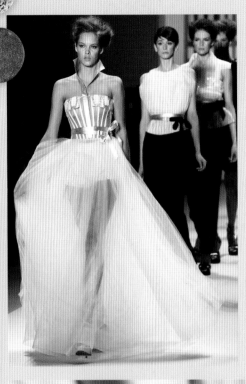

► NATURAL WONDER
Nature is an endless source of shapes and patterns. The petals of a red rose might inspire the shape and structure of frills or ruffles on a dress.

◄▼ INSPIRED BY SCIENCE
Scientific and nature books and magazines are a good source of ideas. Close-up images are distorted and unexpected details may be revealed. Imagine how this bee's translucent wing could be translated into the sheer skirts of a dress.

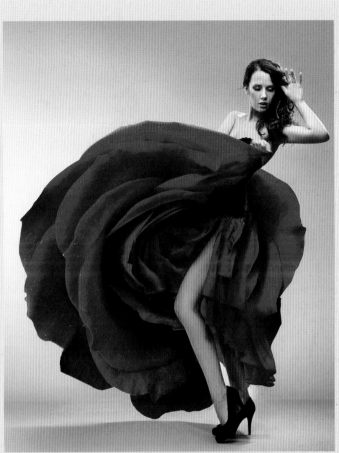

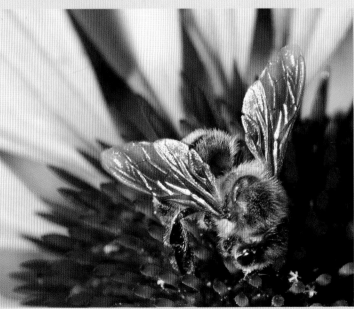

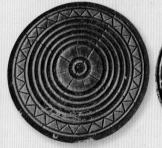

▲► LAYERS OF POSSIBILITY
Repetitive man-made patterns can inspire print designs; look a little closer and layers of rust or discoloration may evoke ideas about fabric layering.

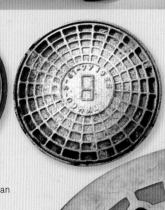

UNIT 7 Designing fabric ideas

The close examination of the surface detail of your source of inspiration can stimulate exciting ideas about textures and colors, which will influence your choice of fabrics. Instead of relying on fabrics that you can buy, you might decide that you want to design your own textiles, using methods such as embroidery, dyeing, knitting, or printing. These original textiles can then be incorporated into truly unique garment designs. As a general rule, when you let your ornate textile ideas take the lead, your garment designs

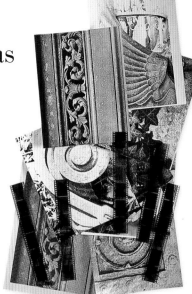

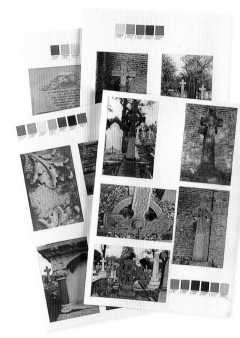

◀▼ **RAPID RESEARCH**
Photography is a great way to quickly gather useful research. Using a black-and-white mode will help focus your mind on texture and linear pattern, whereas color photography can provide you with a good starting point for your color palette.

the project
Choose a theme that allows the examination of detail and would be suitable to inspire interesting textile ideas. Explore your concept through drawings or photography. Use a mood board to help you select a color palette and finalize your fabric ideas. Choose the strongest textile concepts and let them inspire some simple fashion designs that display the fabric ideas in their best light.

the objective
● Select an appropriate starting point for textile development.
● Expand your ideas about creating different fabrics.
● Assess your strongest

fabric concepts to inspire your rough fashion designs.

the process
Choose a promising theme to research; an old graveyard, for example, offers many interesting textural details such as carved stonework, rusty railings, and layered leaves. Photography is a good way to gather research quickly. You can view your subject as an overall scene or in close-up, and the very act of looking through the viewfinder will give you a fresh perspective. Then make further sketches either on site or later, in the studio, using the photographs as reference. You can also digitally edit the photographs, scanning

images into a computer and using software packages such as Adobe Photoshop to manipulate scale and color.

Group together your color photographs and create color palettes by selecting the important shades and identifying the harmonious combinations (see page 118). Alternatively, limiting yourself to black-and-white photography will help you focus on shapes and textures.

Consider how your research themes would be translated onto fabric. You can embellish fabrics through methods such as cutting, bleaching, painting, dyeing, printing, beading, or appliqué. You could even design an idea for an entirely new textile,

generated through knitting, for example. Use a mood board as a focus, gathering any trims, beads, ribbons, or print effects that you may wish to use.

Finally, sketch some fashion designs that show off your textile ideas to best advantage. Remember that an intricate fabric is often best shown in a simple garment shape.

SEE ALSO
● Mood boards, p. 28
● Starting with embroidery, p. 52
● Structuring fabric, p. 122

► TRYING OUT IDEAS
Start to sketch your rough garment ideas, incorporating fabric ideas that reflect the shapes and patterns of your research material. Try placing the fabric concepts on a figure in different scales and proportions.

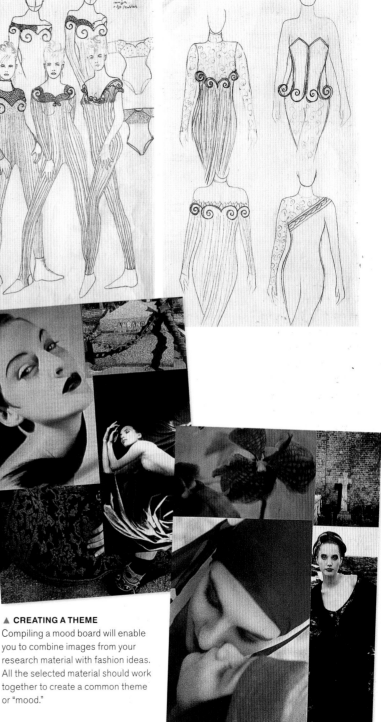

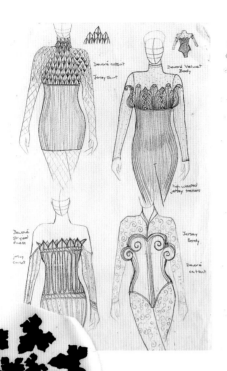

◄ SIMPLICITY IN DESIGN
Simplify images, such as representations of overlapping leaves, down to repetitive patterns that can be used in a decorative way. These prints were inspired by art nouveau examples of leaf designs.

SELF-CRITIQUE
- Was your chosen source of inspiration sufficiently detailed to inspire textile ideas?
- Have you expanded from the original starting point to create unique textile designs?
- Have you used the strongest textile ideas in your rough garment designs?

▲ CREATING A THEME
Compiling a mood board will enable you to combine images from your research material with fashion ideas. All the selected material should work together to create a common theme or "mood."

UNIT 7 Designing fabric ideas

should become simpler to let the beauty of the fabric be seen and appreciated.

Developing a fabric concept in conjunction with a garment design allows for total control of the creative process—giving a designer the opportunity to produce a truly original collection that reflects the research material in a unique way. To give designs a strong overall look, the inspiration of the source should be shown in different ways. For example, it is not just the surface treatment of the fabrics that strongly reflects the theme in the garments illustrated here—even the poses of the figures are reminiscent of the graveyard source.

Here, the simple fashion shapes are a suitable vehicle for displaying the fabric ideas. When designers invest a great deal of effort into creating a beautiful fabric, they tend to keep outlines as simple as possible. An elaborate silhouette combined with a complex textile can lead to a confused overall effect. Conversely, the illustration of the textile should not be so over-the-top that it detracts from the silhouette. For clarity, garment designs can always be presented accompanied by fabric swatches or separate textile illustrations.

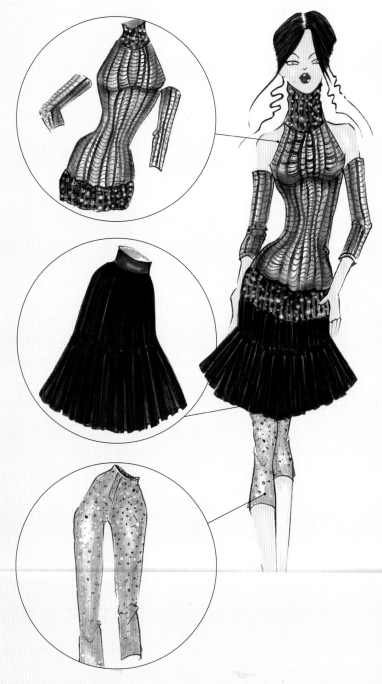

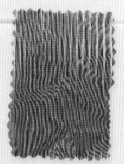
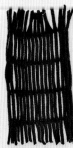

◀▶ PULLING IT TOGETHER
The range is coordinated by the anchor factors of similar fabric, trim (beading, metallics, and embroidery), and body-conscious silhouettes. The items in this range can all be interchanged for multiple looks.

▼▶ BALANCED DESIGNS

The style of the final illustrations can also help to evoke the source. Here the figure has been treated in a static, statuesque manner reminiscent of the graveyard sculptures. The fabric and silhouette also work in harmony: simple outlines allow textiles to speak for themselves, and the depiction of the textile does not overwhelm the presentation of the garment as a whole.

Creating clean silhouettes comprised of interesting lace or embroidered fabric will update a classic silhouette. This princess-line dress is a classic silhouette rendered with burn-out velvet.

This asymmetrical lace top paired with a velvet mermaid-length evening skirt coordinates with the other pieces in the range of after-five separates shown here. The beaded gray pants could be substituted for the mermaid skirt.

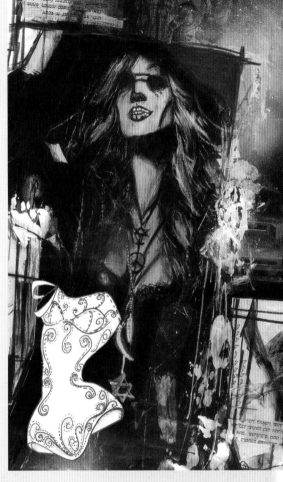

▲ REINFORCING THE TREND MESSAGE

This abstract image uses dark tones and shadows to highlight the mood of "goth glamour." The lace bustier technical flat was overlaid on the illustration to reinforce the trend message.

If you have the technical know-how, you can translate your ideas onto real fabrics. Strong chemicals were used to burn the design into this store-purchased silk velvet.

UNIT 8 Starting with embroidery

The previous unit demonstrates that fashion design can be driven by fabric development. In the same way, embroidery can be used as the starting point for a garment idea. You can draw on paintings for patterns and shapes to develop into embroidery designs. The artist Gustav Klimt, for example, used intricate and ornate patterns, and his work would be an ideal starting point for this exercise. You may have your own preference, but be sure to choose a source that contains sufficient decorative information to inspire you throughout your investigations. Look for shapes and patterns that can be simplified and adapted to your own design ends.

As you incorporate your embroidery ideas into garment designs, take your lead from the pages of fashion magazines. You will notice that the size, amount, and placement of embroidery used by

▶ **PATTERN AND RHYTHM**
Choose images that demonstrate a strong sense of pattern and rhythm, like these two paintings by Gustav Klimt. The swirling shapes are ideal for translating into an embroidered design.

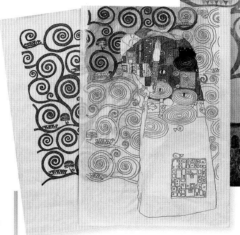

the project
Select a work of art that you find inspiring. Explore the patterns, colors, and shapes of the chosen piece, using painting, drawing, photography, gathered research, and fashion magazine cuttings. As you work, gradually isolate simple patterns and shapes that are easily interpreted into embroidery, and use these to inspire fashion designs.

the objective
● Select a suitable starting point for embroidery development.

● Combine textile and garment design by using intricate ornamentation in a fashion context.
● Select your strongest embroidery ideas to inspire your fashion designs.

▲ ▶ ▼ **WIDENING YOUR INVESTIGATIONS**
Use a sketchbook to explore patterns from paintings. Create mood boards combining research from magazines with your sketches to support your observations of an artist's work, and develop simple decorative patterns. Look out for patterns to photograph. The wrought-iron work, below, continues the decorative theme.

SELF-CRITIQUE
● Was your chosen source of inspiration suitably detailed for the development of embroidery as well as fashion ideas?
● Did you let your decorative concept take the lead in the garment design, balancing intricate ornamentation with simple design?
● Have you taken the strongest ideas through to rough sketch stage?

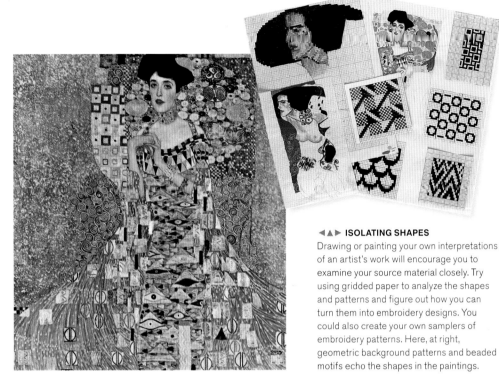

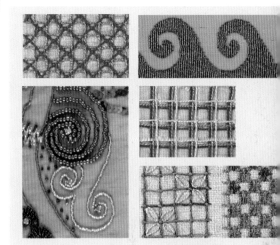

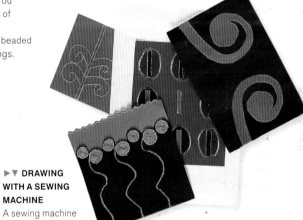

◀▲▶ ISOLATING SHAPES

Drawing or painting your own interpretations of an artist's work will encourage you to examine your source material closely. Try using gridded paper to analyze the shapes and patterns and figure out how you can turn them into embroidery designs. You could also create your own samplers of embroidery patterns. Here, at right, geometric background patterns and beaded motifs echo the shapes in the paintings.

the process

Begin by looking at the work of your chosen artist, but stay focused by editing down the starting points. Careful selection is vital to the design process. You might wish to combine your research with photographs of your own that capture similar patterns. This primary research adds originality to your design solutions—but keep it simple.

Draw or paint your own interpretations of the work, evolving these into simplified patterns and shapes. Use collage and machine embroidery to begin developing decorative ideas. Echo the shapes and patterns that you have observed. These pieces are drawings, too, but they're done with a sewing machine rather than a pen!

Begin by using the colors of your source material, but feel free to move away into your own palette. Changing colors can give a new twist to a familiar pattern.

Now work your embroidery ideas into some garment designs. Remember that a simple garment shape will show off embroidery to best effect. Pockets, collars, necklines, hems, and cuffs can all be good places to site decoration, or you might want to be bolder and place a design within the front or back bodice or on a sleeve. Decoration can be used once or repeated over the garment, in a random or engineered pattern. At this stage, you should also reconsider your choice of colors and make the palette appropriate to your target customer. Select your strongest ideas to pull together as the final fashion designs.

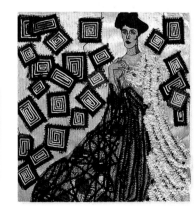

▶▼ DRAWING WITH A SEWING MACHINE

A sewing machine can become a tool for drawing. Here, colored paper has been sewn together with different combinations of threads, stitches, colors, and shapes.

SEE ALSO

- Visiting a museum, p. 18
- Fine art and graphics, p. 42
- Small details, big ideas, p. 46
- Designing fabric ideas, p. 48

UNIT 8 Starting with embroidery

designers tend to vary as fashion changes through the seasons. Embroidery ideas can be translated directly onto fabric and used with fashion designs as appropriate, or they can be developed further as print ideas or textures for knitted stitches. It is possible to combine a number of these techniques, embroidering into a print idea or printing over a knit, for example. It might be that a collection contains a mixture, so that some garments are printed whereas others are knitted or embroidered—but they should all reflect, even if it is only distantly, the essential elements of the initial research.

The final garment designs illustrated here have evolved a long way from the initial starting point, and references to Klimt have become subtle. It is important that the finished collection has been shaped by the designer's own sense of style, and reflects the source without being overwhelmed by it.

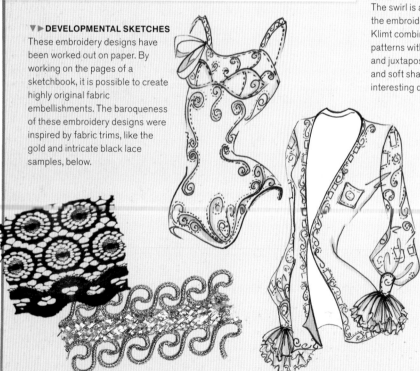

▼▶ DEVELOPMENTAL SKETCHES
These embroidery designs have been worked out on paper. By working on the pages of a sketchbook, it is possible to create highly original fabric embellishments. The baroqueness of these embroidery designs were inspired by fabric trims, like the gold and intricate black lace samples, below.

▼▶ THEMED OUTLINE
The curves and swirls of the source materials are reflected in the silhouettes and trim of the garments sketched here. The swirl is also carried into the embroidery detail. Gustav Klimt combined geometric patterns with curvilinear lines, and juxtaposing these hard and soft shapes can create interesting design concepts.

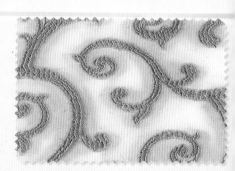

▶ EMBROIDERY AS INSPIRATION FOR TEXTILE PATTERN
Embroidery ideas can be echoed in knitted structures or print designs, as in the printed textile examples here.

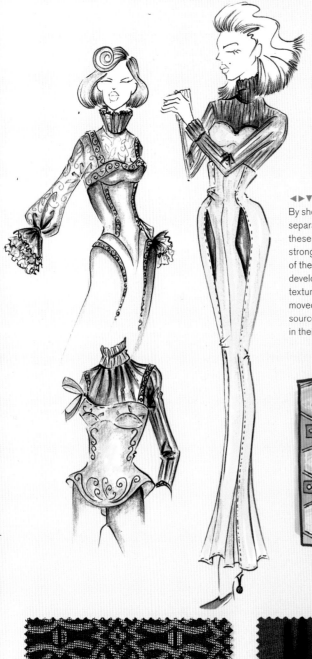

◄▶▼ **COMMUNICATING CLEARLY**
By showing the decorative detail separately from the garment itself, these final illustrations can make a strong statement about both. Some of the embroidery ideas have been developed further into knitted textures. These designs have moved away from the original source to become strong concepts in their own right.

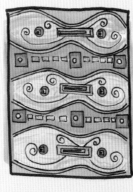

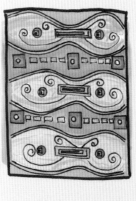

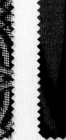

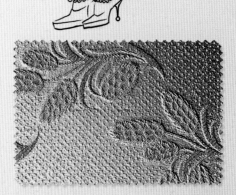

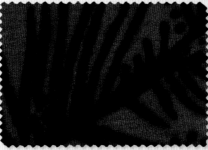

2 Illustrating fashion

Now that you have developed some great design ideas, it's time to look more closely at the techniques of fashion illustration. This chapter discusses creating figures, whether through an easy paper-folding method or by drawing from life, as well as exploring the wide range of media that you can use in illustrating designs and looking at how to lay out your page effectively. Throughout this part of the course, you will learn to observe carefully and to represent what you see in a bold and individual way.

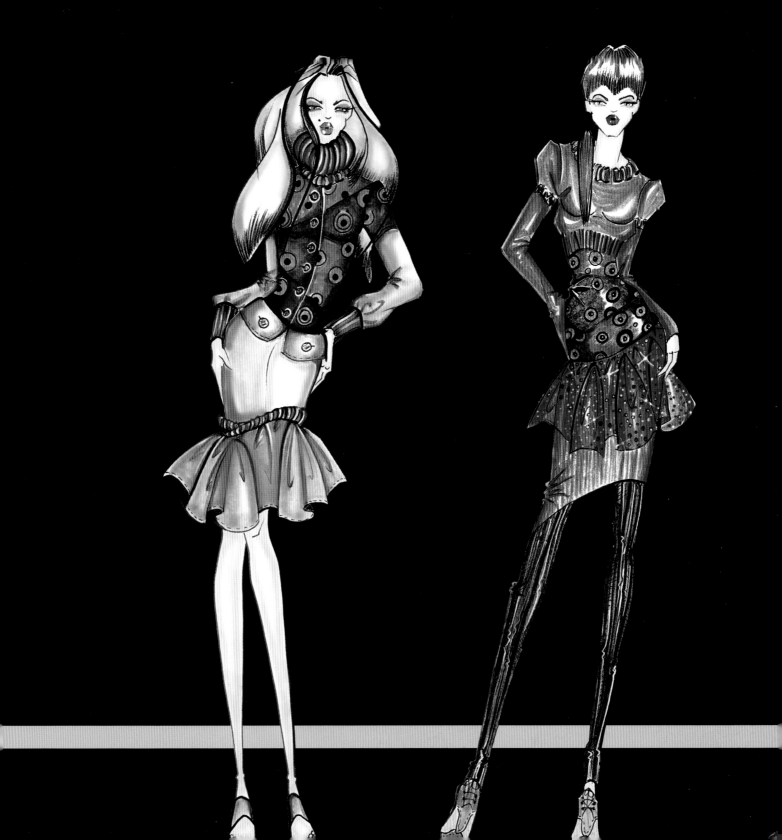

* Drawing in a fast, fluid style is desirable for fashion artists, and is unique to fashion.

* Practice drawing every day, and you will be amazed at how quickly you will improve.

* Look at shapes and proportions before focusing on small details.

Experiments with media

One of the most important aspects of design drawing is the ability to "loosen up." Often a budding designer will freeze up over an important drawing, whether it's for presentation, publication, or just to show to someone else. Spontaneity is lost and any freedom that existed in the private sketchbook can suddenly become rigid and dull.

We can all be a little self-conscious, and fashion is known as an intimidating industry. However, a bold, fluid illustration is more likely to sell a concept or design than an overworked, timid sketch. Confidence and commitment are essential to successful design presentation. Daily quick sketching exercises allow you to practice boldness and are the best method for improvement. Give yourself a short time to complete each sketch—30-second sketches are best for this exercise. Experimenting with different approaches and mediums can also be an aid to improvement, so

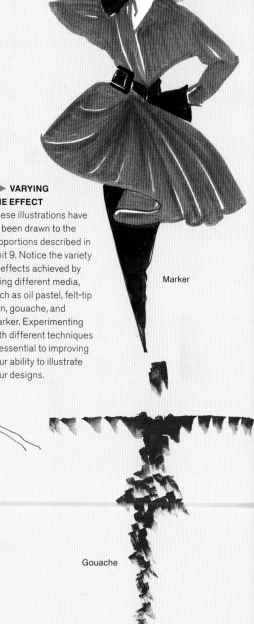

Marker

▼▶ **VARYING THE EFFECT**
These illustrations have all been drawn to the proportions described in Unit 9. Notice the variety of effects achieved by using different media, such as oil pastel, felt-tip pen, gouache, and marker. Experimenting with different techniques is essential to improving your ability to illustrate your designs.

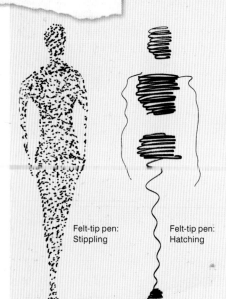

Felt-tip pen: Stippling

Felt-tip pen: Hatching

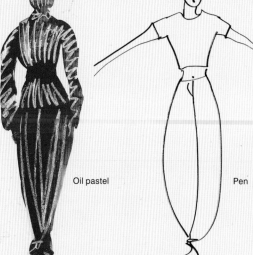

Oil pastel

Pen

Gouache

try changing pad size and techniques. Even if you return to your usual methods after the exercise, the experience of exploration will bring confidence and quicker, fluid lines to your drawings.

Many of these experimental attempts are destined for the trash. However, don't despair, but persevere using a variety of media; pen, ink, watercolor, markers, and different paper supports are all readily available. One fun exercise is to quickly sketch a friend, magazine image, photograph, or reflection in the mirror. Resist the natural impulse to look at the paper, and complete the sketch without lifting your hand from it. The results will vary, but your observation skills will be enhanced. You can also experiment with loose gesture drawing and even doodles and scribbles. These quick sketches will achieve a free and fluid line quality. Don't be too concerned initially about the final outcome, because this is a learning process, and speed and accuracy can be developed later.

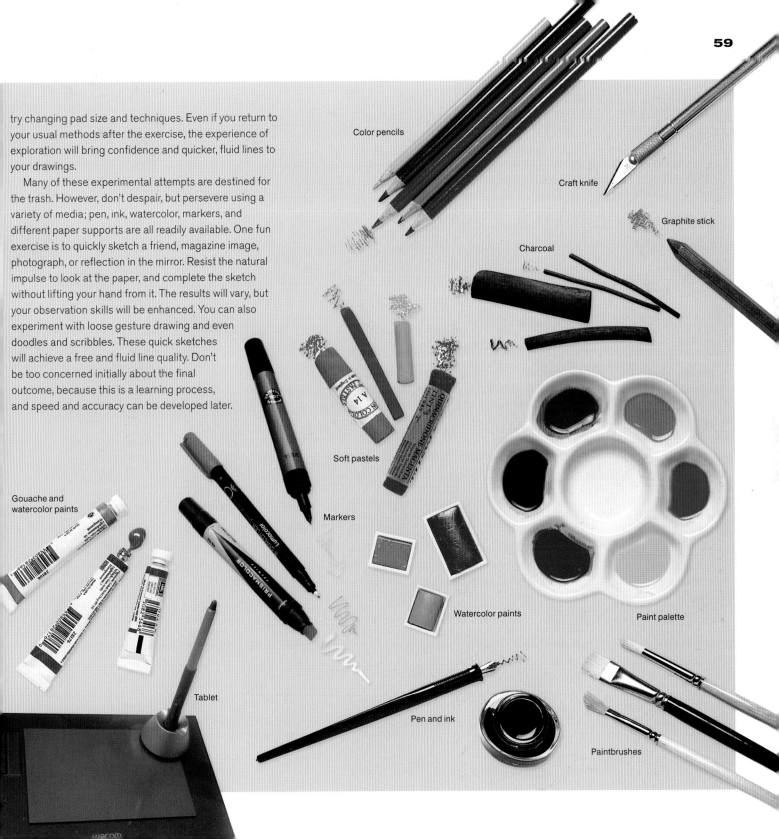

Color pencils

Craft knife

Graphite stick

Charcoal

Soft pastels

Gouache and watercolor paints

Markers

Watercolor paints

Paint palette

Tablet

Pen and ink

Paintbrushes

UNIT 9 An exercise in figure drawing

If you are inexperienced in drawing figures, using this easy method can add to the confidence of your illustrations by ensuring that your figures are roughly in proportion and all drawn to the same scale. The simple shapes and proportions of the method ensure that the figures are easy to draw and look correct. Furthermore, by grasping how these basic shapes fit together to form a human figure, your drawings will become better anchored on the page and the poses more convincing. For the sake of this exercise, the body, broken into its component parts, remains unclothed.

After you have completed the task, you should keep the drawings as a reference. You can always come back to this book, but nothing stays in the memory better than

the project

To use a simple dividing method to make a proportional blueprint of the human figure. The paper is divided into ten equal units, with each unit representing a section of the body. The barometer or unit of measurement is based on the initial head size. Basic block shapes that represent different parts of the body make an easy reference tool for creating future fashion drawings.

tho objoctivo

- Gain a structural framework to strengthen and liberate the creative aspects of your fashion designs.
- Practice drawing and blocking out an elongated figure for

fashion sketches.
- Understanding the basic proportions and shapes of the fashion croquis.

the process

The human body is remarkably consistent in the way it can be divided into equal sections. These sections can be easily understood when the head is used as the barometer or unit of measurement. Fashion figure proportions, like fashion design itself, change over time. However, today's fashion figures are approximately nine to ten heads long. If the figure is wearing flat shoes, then it should be about nine heads; but, because most fashion figures wear high heels, the figure will be further elongated to about ten heads high. Of course,

these are approximations and the length can vary. To start, make a mark just below the top of a sheet of A4 paper. Draw a straight line, the plumb line, down from the top, ending approximately ½ in. (1.3 cm) from the bottom of the paper. Measure the line and divide that measurement into ten equal sections. Draw a notch on the line indicating where each section begins and ends.

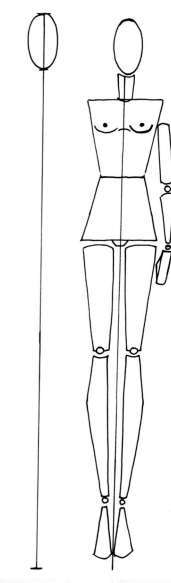

▲ FIGURE
DRAWING METHOD
Once you have drawn and divided a line into ten equal sections as described, you can begin to sketch in the figure with standard body shapes. This exercise will enable you to achieve a correctly proportioned figure.

SELF-CRITIQUE
- Have you followed this exercise step by step?
- Have you gained a better understanding of the basic shapes and proportions that form the fashion figure?
- Will this anatomical knowledge aid your future fashion designs?

Now you are ready to fill in the shapes that will create the proportional human figure. Draw a tapered egg shape from the first mark at the top of the paper to the first notch. Halfway between the first and second notches draw a horizontal line to create the shoulders. At the second notch, place two small dots to indicate the bust apex. The bust apex is approximately one head in width. Next, place another horizontal line at the third notch; this line is approximately the same width as the bust apex. Connect your lines to form a tapered rectangle, creating the upper torso of the body.

Draw another tapered rectangle from the third to the fourth notch, forming the hip box shape. Another small mark placed just beneath the hip line will indicate the crotch. Draw two small balls for the knees at notch six. Draw cylinder shapes to form arms and upper legs.

The lower legs are slightly extended at the seventh notch; this will

form a calf muscle. Place another two small balls for the ankles at the bottom of the legs. Draw in triangle shapes for feet. The foot is equal to one head.

To complete your figure, sketch in a neck

cylinder shape, slender hand blocks, and half circles at the bust line. You now have an elongated fashion figure that can be used as a template for your designs.

▼ MANIPULATING THE BASIC FORMS
This sequence of drawings shows how lines and shapes created using the method described here can be developed into more formal final illustrations. The basic shapes and structure of these gesture sketches remain in proportion. These quick drawings can be manipulated and the limbs rotated to create a sense of animation and movement.

SEE ALSO
● The human body in proportion, p. 64

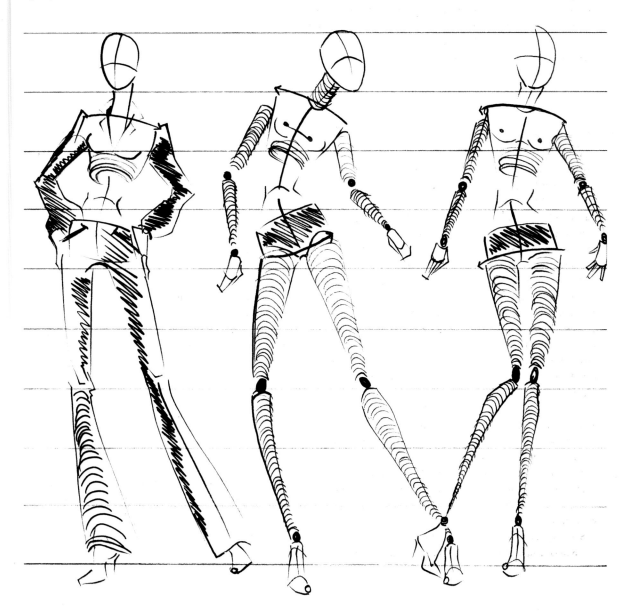

UNIT 9 An exercise in figure drawing

something learned by actually doing it yourself and, once you have mastered the project on these pages, you'll soon be able to draw figures instinctively.

Although it is essential for a fashion designer to strive to break new ground and sometimes disregard conventions, it is nevertheless also useful to be grounded in a few basic design principles. It is important for designers always to keep in mind the fact that, whatever flights of fancy they may be exploring, their garments will eventually have to fit on a human body.

In fashion illustration, it is usual to stretch the legs a little, particularly below the calf, but all other body parts must also be elongated in proportion to the legs to create an elegant and proportional body. The simple figure drawing method shown on page 60 achieves a pattern for a fashionably elongated, but correctly proportioned, figure that can be used as a foundation for illustrations. It is always possible to break completely with convention, but a student should start with a framework to support the free ideas that might follow. It is only once the basic principles have been absorbed that a designer can enjoy true artistic freedom.

▶ **TAKING LIBERTIES**
Because the basic structure of these figures is correct, the designer has been able to emphasize key style points. The garments have been exaggerated at the shoulders, waist, and legs, creating a cohesive look. These are considered "working drawings," and are possible when the under structure is created first and a rough figure is blocked out. An overlay is then drawn on a separate piece of paper showing the clothing.

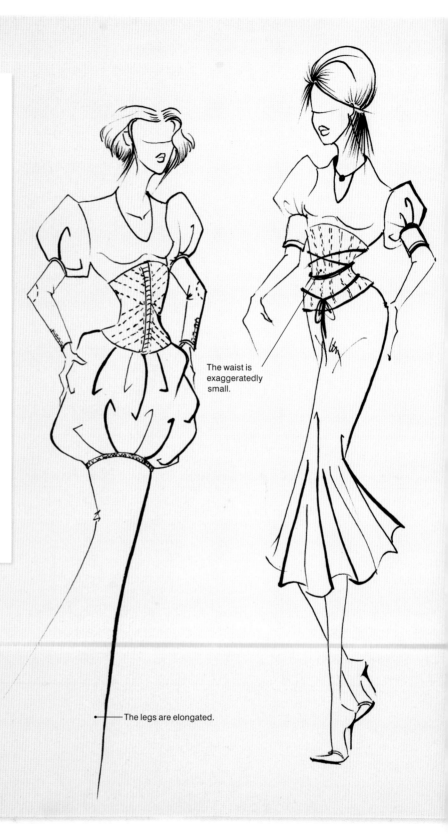

The waist is exaggeratedly small.

The legs are elongated.

▶ **HIDDEN STRUCTURE**

These marker drawings were all created using the hidden structure or block figure as a template to draw over. This template and the progressive drawing over the top is called an overlay. An overlay can be rendered with marker once the structure is developed and the clothing drawn as line art.

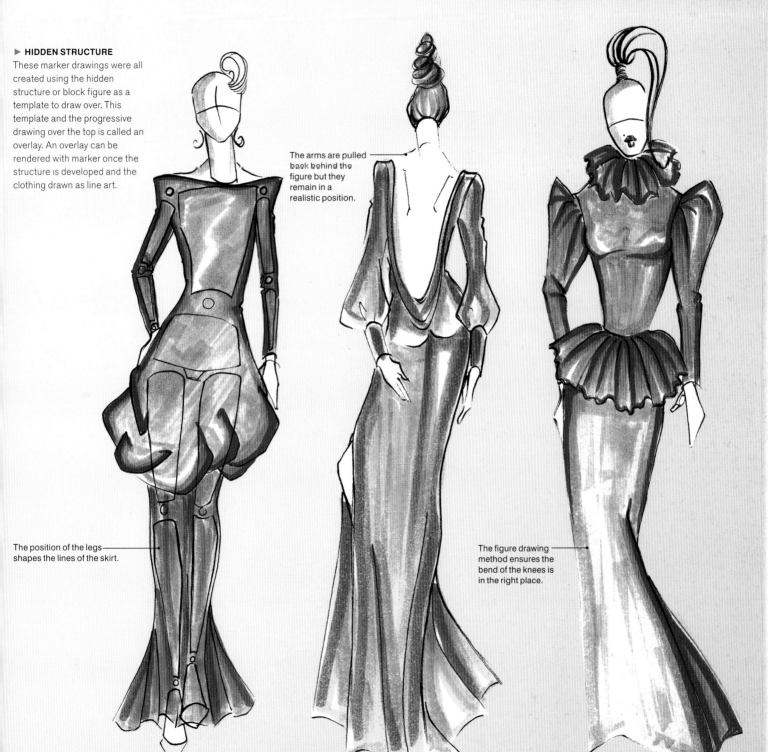

The arms are pulled back behind the figure but they remain in a realistic position.

The position of the legs shapes the lines of the skirt.

The figure drawing method ensures the bend of the knees is in the right place.

* Give yourself a good grounding in drawing the human body. This will help you to understand the mechanics of the body.

* Fashion figures are often elongated, with particularly long legs, but their bodies should still be correctly proportioned.

The human body in proportion

As a fashion designer, you should always remember that clothes are made to be worn by real people. It is important, therefore, to gain some understanding of the structure and proportions of the human body.

▼ SHAPES IN THE FIGURE

Simple shapes are used to create the fashion figure. The head is portrayed as an egg; the chest a tapered rectangle; the pelvic hip box another tapered rectangle; the limbs as cylinders; feet and hands as blocks or triangles; and small balls can represent bones and joints.

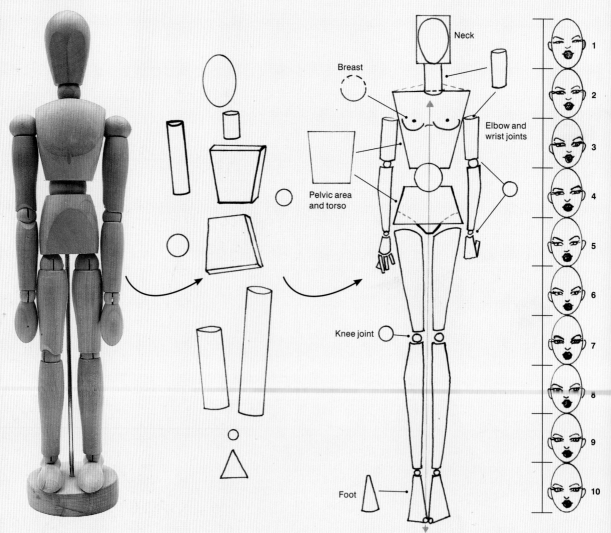

Neck

Breast

Elbow and wrist joints

Pelvic area and torso

Knee joint

Foot

▶ FIGURE DRAWING

Artists' wooden articulated figures can help you to break down the human figure into simple shapes which, combined with the figure drawing method on page 60, provide an easy method for drawing a realistic figure.

The exercise in figure drawing described on page 60 will introduce you to a simple and easy system that you can use to draw figures that are roughly in proportion. The exercise has nothing to do with creativity, but will help you grasp the possibilities and restrictions of the framework on which your creations will hang.

There are obvious differences in the male and female forms, such as narrower waists and wider hips for females and squarer chests and faces for men. However, these variations should be incorporated once the basics have been sketched. Male and female bodies can both be broken down into the same simple block shapes. The head can be portrayed as an egg; the chest as a wastepaper basket; the pelvic area as a wide gymnastic vaulting horse; the limbs as tapering tubes; the feet and hands as cones; and the joints as balls. Once you have drawn these shapes in the relative sizes shown (opposite), in a straightforward front view, you can move them around like parts of a wooden drawing dummy to create the pose you want.

There is a convention in fashion illustration that a figure should be elongated to give it more elegance. Although most elongation occurs in the legs, specifically below the knee, the entire figure should be elongated to create a proportional body. For example, not elongating the neck and the arms will create a stumpy looking upper body. When drawing the female figure for fashion, the goal is to create an elegant and slender body, and that can be achieved by elongating the neck, the arms, the torso just a little, and the legs.

When you come to draw from life, a grasp of these principles will help you enormously in understanding the mechanics of the figure in front of you. It is always good to remember that these "rules" are just conventions, but by gaining a basic understanding of the structure and proportions of the human body, you will be better placed to break the rules later.

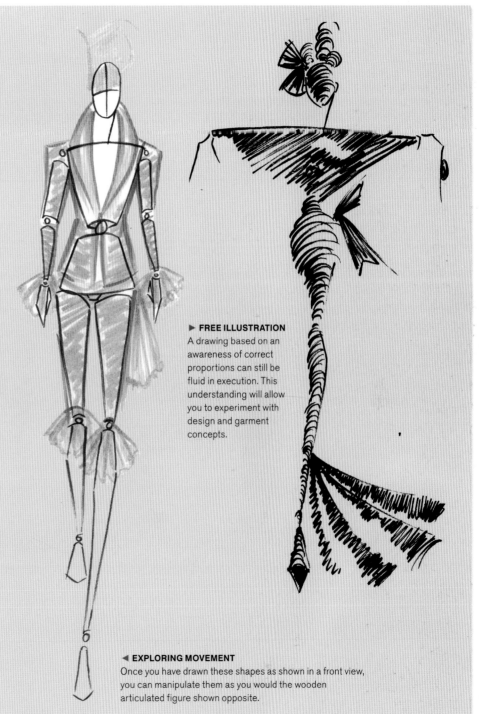

▶ **FREE ILLUSTRATION**
A drawing based on an awareness of correct proportions can still be fluid in execution. This understanding will allow you to experiment with design and garment concepts.

◀ **EXPLORING MOVEMENT**
Once you have drawn these shapes as shown in a front view, you can manipulate them as you would the wooden articulated figure shown opposite.

UNIT 10 Drawing from life

It cannot be stressed too strongly that if you are designing clothes, however exotic your sources, you must always remember that at the end of the day you are designing for a human body. Practicing life drawing is therefore a very valuable exercise that will help you observe clearly and assess quickly what you see. Using a model means you do not have to invent anything out of thin air. The information is in front of you—all you need to do is interpret it in your own individual style.

You may have the opportunity to draw from life in an art school environment, but you can also improvise if you are working at home by asking a friend to pose. There is no need for your model to be fashionably dressed. Normal daywear with a few additional accessories, such as hats, scarves, boots, or sunglasses, is quite sufficient. It is more important for the class tutor, or

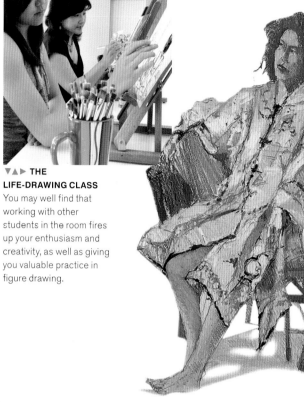

▼▲▶ **THE LIFE-DRAWING CLASS**
You may well find that working with other students in the room fires up your enthusiasm and creativity, as well as giving you valuable practice in figure drawing.

SEE ALSO
- An exercise in figure drawing, p. 60
- Learn to love your roughs, p. 94

the project
Spend a day practicing life drawing either in class with a professional model or at home having persuaded a friend to pose for you. If you choose the private route, there are bound to be some giggles at the outset, That is not a problem—the exercise should be fun. Try to achieve fifteen drawings by the end of the session, spending no more than two to five minutes on each drawing.

the objective
- Make over reality in your own style.
- Improve your ability to work fast and to observe quickly and carefully.
- Achieve freshness and boldness in illustration by getting the poses down on paper as quickly as possible.
- Capture the spirit of the garments while representing them graphically.

the process
First, spend a few minutes drawing the pose and the garment outlines in what you consider to be your own style. Be bold. Quickly capturing the pose, you have to assess the essentials and get them down on paper very fast. Avoid making feeble, sketchy pencil marks that result in tentative "hairy-lined" outlines.

Next, try not to look at your paper, and make a continuous line drawing, without removing the pencil from the paper. Keep the poses changing every few minutes. Now you can use some paints, choosing just three or four colors. Apply the color with a broad brush, jotting

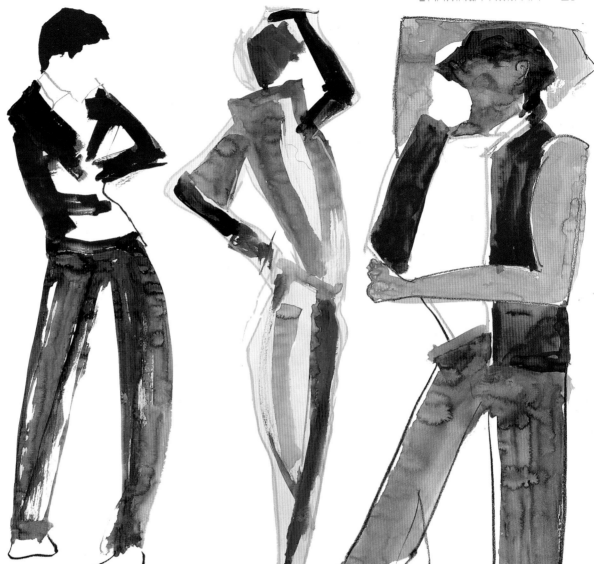

► CAPTURING THE POSES
These figures were illustrated during a life-drawing class. The limited time available to complete each pose has resulted in images that capture the essence of the garments and make a strong statement. If you do not have time to worry about getting outlines exactly right, you are more likely to achieve images that are fluid and full of life and spontaneity.

down the poses with quick brushstrokes.

Now you can start mixing your media. Perhaps begin by representing the clothes in paint, but use crayon or oil pastel to delineate the facial features.

Remember to try to make each drawing fill the whole page, and exaggerate the poses to bring drama to the illustrations. Sometimes it can be productive to ask the model to adopt unusual poses, either seated, standing, or draped over a prop (which you may wish either to

include or leave out in order to make use of the white space left on the page). However, be sure that the pose does not interfere with the communication of your ideas.

SELF-CRITIQUE
● Did you observe the model fully?
● Were the poses interesting?
● Has the exercise speeded up and sharpened your observational techniques?

UNIT 10 Drawing from life

you if you are working at home, to persuade the model to exaggerate the poses, and to change them often. Accentuation adds drama to the drawings, and responding quickly to the changing poses will bring spontaneity to your work.

One of the most stimulating aspects of working with a life model is having to use every second of the session to the best advantage. The challenge of responding quickly to fast-changing poses brings spontaneity to the resultant drawings. A bold commitment can make any drawing compelling.

These figures were drawn to fill the whole page, with the model's extreme poses exaggerated to bring energy to the illustrations. The confident use of different media, such as markers or pastels, can bring excitement to a quickly drawn illustration. Try to capture the mood and active stance of the model, and work quickly to achieve fresh, fluid lines.

▶ **EXPLOITING COLOR AND MEDIUM**
These illustrations use both color and medium to good effect. The limited palette has ensured an emphasis on the silhouettes, using felt pen, pencils, and wash. The essence of each pose has been swiftly identified and captured on paper.

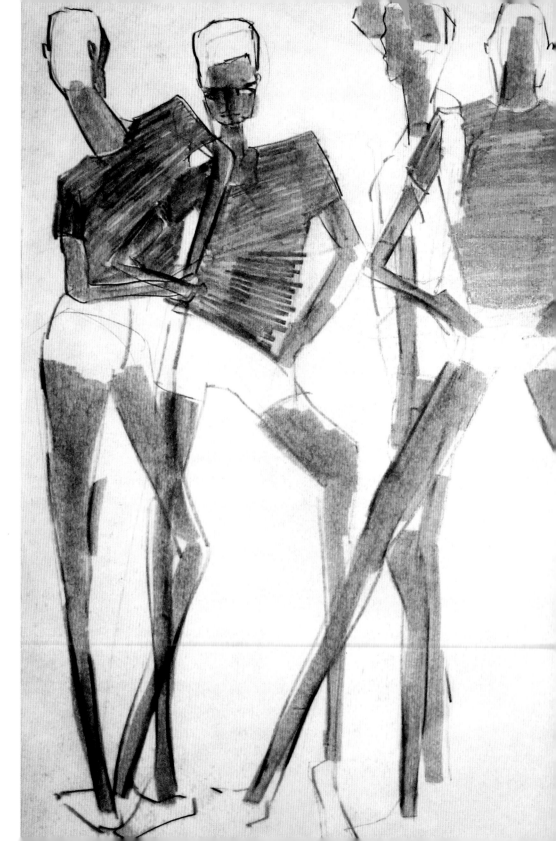

◀▼ USING ARTIST'S MANNEQUINS
A wooden articulated artist's mannequin will help you draw figures accurately and in credible poses. Observe where the figure bends and how the body shapes relate to each other, and start to make sketches, starting with the largest shapes. An anatomical underdrawing will give you a better understanding of body structure and will make your clothed figures more realistic.

▲▶ HANDS ON HIPS
A figure's attitude and personality is communicated first and foremost by its body language. The basic "hands on hips" pose of the mannequin (above) is transformed into a confident and proud character when color and facial detail are applied to the pencil underdrawing.

▲▶ STRIKING A POSE
This is a difficult pose to draw well. Pose your artist's mannequin first, and make some basic line drawings to really get a feel for the movement implicit in the pose.

▲▶ ON THE RUNWAY
Capturing a figure mid-runway is something you will have to do time and time again. Movement is key to your success and, while an artist's mannequin won't help you with this, it will provide you with the basic anatomical detail to get the walking pose correct.

UNIT 11 Digital illustration

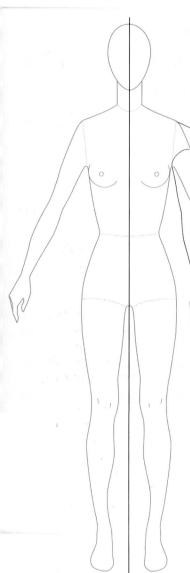

▲ **BASE CROQUIS**
You can use a base croquis for the development of flats. The croquis is used as a guideline for drawing garments as well as for creating pieces that are uniform in size and proportion.

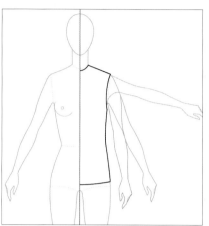

▲ **DUPLICATING GARMENT PARTS**
1. One advantage of using the computer is that many tasks are repeatable, which helps designers save time. Here half of the garment is drawn, and the entire half is then copied in its mirror image to produce a full garment. Select the entire half garment drawn. In the toolbox, double click on the "Reflect" tool, choose "Vertical" axis, and press "Copy." Now you can move the new half to match its complement piece.

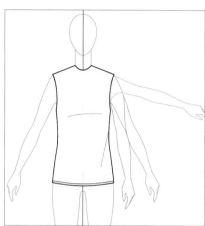

2. Using the "Selection" tool, select the newly created half, hold the shift key, and drag the piece to create a full garment. Holding the shift key restricts movement on one axis only.

There are a variety of software programs available for digital design. In relation to fashion design and illustration, vector programs (such as Adobe Illustrator) are primarily drawing tools, while raster programs (such as Adobe Photoshop) are primarily painting tools. However, each of these programs can perform a huge variety of functions.

Vector software
Vector image is based on a line (or curve) segment between two different points. A collection of these lines and curves produces a vector object. When you hear the word vector, think in terms of crisp, clean lines. These graphics are space-efficient, and enlarging them does not affect quality, because details of the image are preserved. The software uses mathematical formulas to enlarge the image. These applications are great for drawing flats, creating repeat fabric patterns, using text fonts, and creating logos. Common examples are Adobe Illustrator and Corel Draw.

Raster software
Raster images are created through the incorporation of small dots or squares (called pixels) on a given surface area (dots per inch or dpi). Here you need to think in terms of resolution and file size, which are inversible. As the image is enlarged, these squares and the empty spaces between them become more visible, and the picture becomes less clear, with a rough edge. The

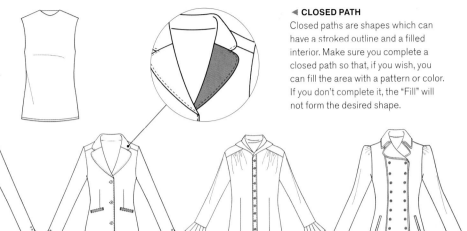

▼▶ EVOLUTION OF A BASIC GARMENT

You can use Adobe Illustrator to modify an existing garment, such as the basic sleeveless top (right), and to create new garments. Various design elements, such as collars, pockets, cuffs, sleeves, and fastenings, can be added, saving time redrawing each piece from scratch. Such design elements can be saved in a digital library file for future access.

◀ CLOSED PATH

Closed paths are shapes which can have a stroked outline and a filled interior. Make sure you complete a closed path so that, if you wish, you can fill the area with a pattern or color. If you don't complete it, the "Fill" will not form the desired shape.

the project

Using Adobe Illustrator as your drawing tool, and a standard croquis as a guiding form, draw six relating garments.

the objective

- Learn basic drawing skills in Adobe Illustrator.
- Learn alignment and centering of objects.
- Create a small library of design elements that can be developed further in the future.
- Apply various design elements to a garment to create unique designs.

the process

1 Using Adobe Illustrator and a croquis as guidance, draw a basic sleeveless top. Lock the layer containing the croquis and set its opacity below 100% for ease of drawing—select the croquis and, in "Option bar," lower the opacity. In "Layers palette," lock the croquis layer.

2 Create a new layer. Use the "Pen" tool from the toolbox to draw. Open the "Appearance" palette, go to "Menu bar," then Window>Appearance. Choose your fill as white for silhouette lines and "none" for internal fabric lines and stitchings. Within the "Appearance" palette, you can adjust the path (lines and curves).

3 Draw various design element pieces that will complement this top: Draw two collar variations, two pocket designs, and two different sleeve designs.

4 Make all your pieces closed path.

5 Copy the basic top and paste it five times by selecting the basic top, then in "Menu bar" go to Edit>Copy, Edit>Paste, five times.

6 Add one of your design elements to each top.

7 Merge and group the design element with a basic top. To do this, select the top and its corresponding design element using the "Selection" tool. In "Menu bar" go to Object>Group. The basic top and design element will move as one piece.

8 You should now have six different garments using a base top.

9 Align and center the pieces for a uniform view. Select all of the garments using the "Selection" tool, then in "Options bar" select "Vertical" and "Horizontal distribute."

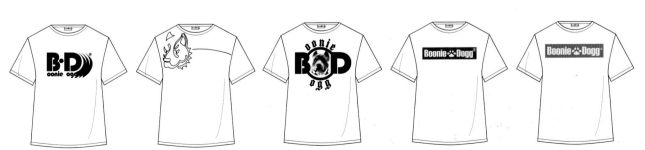

◀ LOGO DESIGN

Using Adobe Illustrator, designers can create logos with clean, crisp lines that can be printed on a variety of company products. These graphics can be enlarged since vector images are resolution independent.

UNIT 11 Digital illustration

more dots/pixels per inch in a given image, the higher the resolution and the clearer the image—but as the resolution grows, so does the size of the file. When scanning an image or fabric for web viewing, a resolution of 150 dpi will suffice; when the aim is to print the image, then a dpi of 300 should be used. Higher dpi scans can be made, but application/software work speed will be affected, and larger file size will mean slower web upload and download speeds.

Raster-based applications are excellent for rendering fabrics, garments, and draped figures, and for creating presentation boards. Common examples are Adobe Photoshop and Corel Paint.

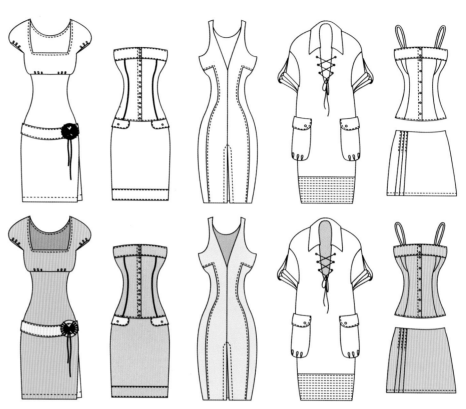

▶ **QUICK COLOR**
When an object is a closed path, like these simple garment illustrations, it can be quickly rendered in color with Adobe Illustrator's "Swatch" panel.

▶ **DIGITAL RENDERING OF FLATS AND FLOATS**
You can create a variety of patterned swatches using Adobe Illustrator. These can then be saved to Illustrator's "Swatches" palette and used to render the closed paths of the same garment outline to create different designs for a portfolio. Turn to page 118 to learn how to create and apply a "seamless" digital pattern.

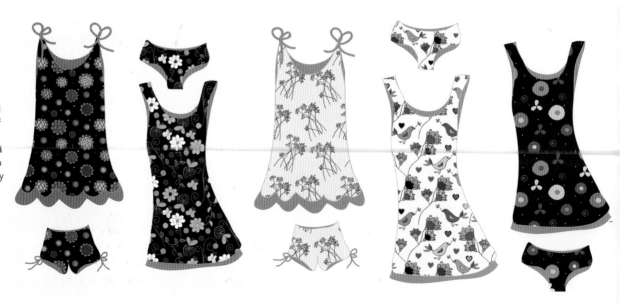

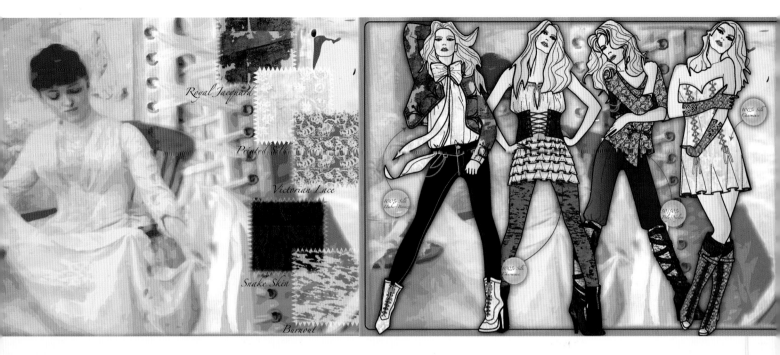

Royal Jacquard

Printed Silk

Victorian Lace

Snake Skin

Burnout

▲ **RENDERING CLOTHED FIGURES**
Adobe Photoshop was used here to render the clothed figures
(right) with the fabric swatches on the mood board (left). While
the lace, silk, and jacquards collection was inspired by the Victorian
era, the modern silhouette makes this collection suitable for
today's woman.

the project

Create a collection of four
figures draped in clothing
geared toward a specific
target customer and, with
the help of Adobe
Photoshop, render your
collection using scanned
fabric swatches.

the objective

- Learn the uses of layers
  in Photoshop.
- Adjust, modify, and
  overlap layers to achieve
  desired fabric effects.
- Learn how to define

fabrics as "Patterns" and
use the "Stamp" tool to
render garments.

the process

1 Design a collection of
  garments and drape them
  on hand-drawn figures or
  croquis templates.
2 Select two to three fabric
  swatches.
3 Scan your drawings and
  fabric swatches to
  Photoshop. Scan figures
  at 300 dpi and fabric
  swatches at 150 dpi.
4 Define each of the

fabrics as a "Pattern":
crop and clean fabric
swatches where
necessary. In "Menu" go
to Edit > Define pattern >
Name pattern.
5 Lock the layer containing
  the figures. This will stop
  you from rendering
  directly on this layer. You
  will create a new layer for
  each garment piece
  layered. This means each
  one can be adjusted and
  manipulated independent
  of the others.
6 Having the locked

draped figure drawing
layer as your active layer,
use the "Magic wand" or
"Lasso" tool from the
toolbox to select a part
you want to render.
7 Click on the "Create new
  layer" icon within the
  "Layers" panel. Name
  your layer. Within the
  "Layers" panel, change
  the "Blending mode" of
  new layer to "Multiply."
8 Choose the "Pattern
  stamp" tool from the
  toolbox, and within
  "Options bar" select the

"Pattern picker." Find the
textile swatch that was
defined as "Pattern"
earlier. Using the
"Pattern stamp" tool
render garment selections
with chosen fabric.
9 Create a new layer for
  each garment and repeat
  the process.
10 Modify each layer's
   "blending mode,"
   "opacity," and "layer
   style," and make
   "adjustments" (Image >
   Adjustments) to achieve
   the desired effect.

UNIT 11 Digital illustration

Keyboard shortcuts

Whenever possible take advantage of digital software shortcuts. When using Adobe Photoshop and Illustrator, there are many keyboard shortcuts available to speed the design process. When working on a long project, every second saved not dragging the mouse around the screen looking for the needed tool or application menu will save you tremendous time cumulatively. As an example, if you hover above each tool within the toolbox, you can see the appropriate keyboard shortcut. When using Photoshop, under menu, go to Window>Workspace>Keyboards and menus. Here you can view and edit keyboard shortcuts. To access and edit keyboard shortcuts

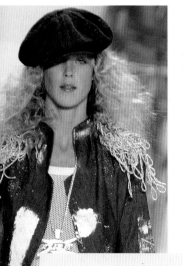

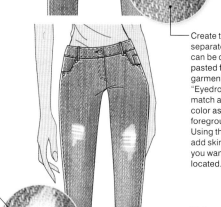

◄▼► **DIGITAL DENIM**
Denim can be scanned and imported into Photoshop to give a quick and easy impression of the fabric. It can then be "distressed" to create rips, tears, and fade marks, and to expose threads.

Create the rip on a separate layer, so it can be copied and pasted for use in other garments. Use the "Eyedropper" tool to match and set the skin color as the foreground color. Using the "Brush" tool, add skin tone where you want the rips to be located.

Use the "Brush" tool to add white horizontal lines, representing the undyed weft-yarn threads.

Distress marks or "whiskering" marks are added using the "Brush" tool. Set the opacity of the color to transparent white. Add marks where the jeans will wear out most quickly.

WHY USE DIGITAL SOFTWARE?

- Eliminates tasks that are labor-intensive, time-consuming, and repetitive by hand.

- Easy sharing—you can E-mail copies of your art work, or post them online.
- No need to take up physical storage space with papers and boards.

- "Delete" and "Undo" options make digital design less prone to mistakes, and allow for the creation of clean, professional designs.

- Using the "Layers" function gives you ultimate flexibility and control over foreground and background images simultaneously.

SEE ALSO

- Digital presentation boards, p. 32
- Digital portfolios, p. 148

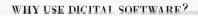

in Adobe Illustrator: Menu>Edit>Keyboard shortcuts. It's also a good idea to search the Internet for different available shortcuts. Some Mac and PC shortcuts are different. Keyboard shortcut web site examples are *http://webdesignerwall.com/tutorials/adobe-illustrator-shortcuts* and *http://webdesignerwall.com/tutorials/photoshop-secret-shortcuts.*

Digital sketchbooks

Now our sketchbooks can also be digital. With a mobile device like an iPad, you can draw and paint on the go and with ease. Artists and fashion designers can jot down ideas on the move, draw and sketch as they get inspired on location, and further develop those digital sketches using traditional digital software. Some modern digital programs are—paradoxically—more primitive, and hence intuitive, than using the traditional pen or brush: the artist can use the tip of a finger to draw, or paint with an infinite variety of colors directly onto the digital canvas. Applications are rapidly developed and updated for computers and mobile devices. Some great applications for digital artists and sketchbookers using iPads are ArtStudio,

SketchBook Pro, Brushes, and miniDraw. Although computers and mobile devices can be expensive, many of the painting and drawing applications designed for them are relatively inexpensive or free.

Moving into the future

Designers can now use software programs that show three-dimensional, realistic garments and draped figures. These programs afford industry professionals a closer proximity to reality, and allow them to virtually view a garment (or a collection) and its drape, before committing to manufacturing the designs. Another advantage of 3D design is the possibility to view the garment on its 360-degree rotation axis—you see much more than just the front and back, as with the 2D design tools. Currently, these programs are limited and expensive; however, as we progress into the digital world of fashion, we'll be seeing more use of 3D digital tools. Autodesk's Maya is a popular 3D program, though the fashion industry uses software that is specifically geared toward 3D fashion design, such as Marvelous Designer 2 or Lectra. Some examples can be seen at *www.marvelousdesigner.com.*

▶ **PERSPECTIVE AND VARIATION**
These figures are dynamic and youthful, and various textiles have been applied to the garments to fabricate the collection. By having some figures larger in the foreground, a sense of perspective has been achieved. You can use the "Free transform" tool to re-size elements, while holding the shift key to constrain proportions.

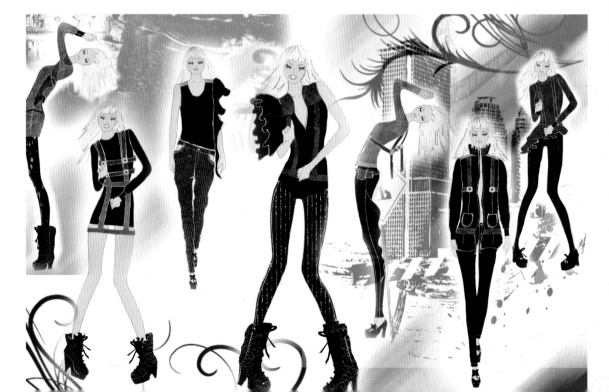

UNIT 12 Exploring collage

SEE ALSO
- Drawing from life, p. 66
- Not just pencil, p. 80
- Laying out your page, p. 84

As a designer, it is essential that you explore all the drawing and rendering tools available to you. One of the more liberating techniques is collage. There are many ways to approach this medium. Colored-paper cutouts, magazines, newsprint, fabrics, and textured papers are all possible materials, while digital collage is another option.

One way of working with collage is to take the technique into the life-drawing studio or classroom. The technique can be adapted for freehand work, or cutout shapes can be applied to the page with a live model at hand to capture the poses in collage. Just as with the life-drawing sessions, working quickly adds spontaneity to the results.

Interesting collages can also be created digitally using a digital camera and Adobe Photoshop. Rough sketches or silhouette outlines can be filled with photographs once you find dynamic or relevant pose concepts, or garments.

More than anything, collage frees you to focus on form, color, and movement, and is an excellent medium for fashion designers. Collage simultaneously

the project

Access a pile of old magazines, photographs, and interesting textured papers. Enlist a friend to model or attend a life-drawing class, and make drawings of your model. Then put together collages that represent the mood and energy of your drawings. Set yourself a limited time to finish each collage—the more challenging the better.

the objective

- Explore new ways of getting abstract ideas down by using the collage medium.
- Free yourself from preconceived ideas of how an image can be used, so that your work will be unique.

the process

Collect plenty of magazine clippings and interesting collage materials to take to a life-drawing session. Quickly draw the model in some active and energetic poses. Select the materials with which you plan to collage the sketch and fill in the drawings by gluing cutout or ripped shapes into the spaces. Try to draw the outer lines of the model and fill in the larger areas first (the head, torso, pelvis, etc.). Think laterally as you work with your material, combining unlikely colors, shapes, and textures. Draw as many silhouettes or outer shapes of the posed model as time will permit.

After the model session, you can play with poses by scanning the sketches into a computer program, such as Photoshop, before compositing these photographs to create a digital collage (as seen in the examples on these pages).

Another method is to print out your digital photographs and cut out interesting shapes. Then glue the shapes to the sketches. Use your imagination to create interesting, appealing outcomes.

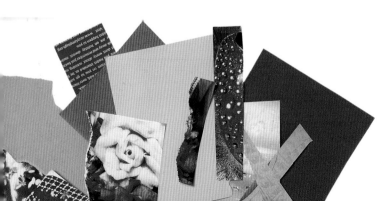

◄ CREATIVE COLLAGE
Magazines can be cut up and wrapping paper can also be used, as can fabric, greeting cards, or digital photographs.

▼ **QUICK THINKING**
Draw quickly from a live model before cutting or
ripping, gluing, or digitally manipulating images
to form interesting collage illustrations.

UNIT 12 Exploring collage

increases your visual vocabulary, and can banish your notions of ordinary expectations.

Exploring different ways to illustrate garments can be liberating for a designer. Although putting pen or marker to paper is the obvious approach, the use of collage can produce particularly intriguing results. The illustrations here make a bold statement: the larger the image, the more compositionally important it will seem.

Collage can work well with more controlled mediums and digital applications. Working with images from the natural world can evoke a surreal feeling. Try a variety of counterintuitive images, and the results may be very compelling.

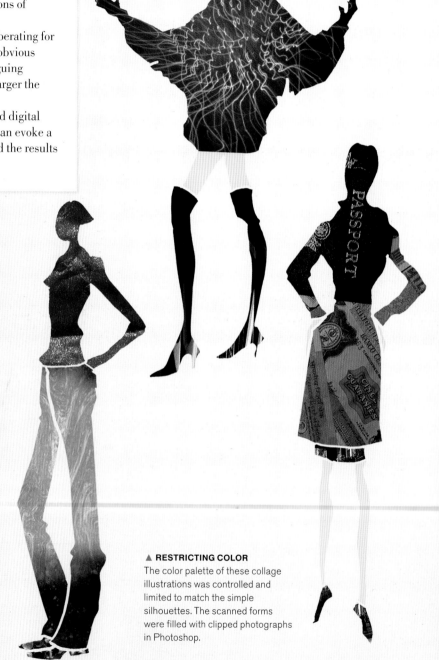

▲ **RESTRICTING COLOR**
The color palette of these collage illustrations was controlled and limited to match the simple silhouettes. The scanned forms were filled with clipped photographs in Photoshop.

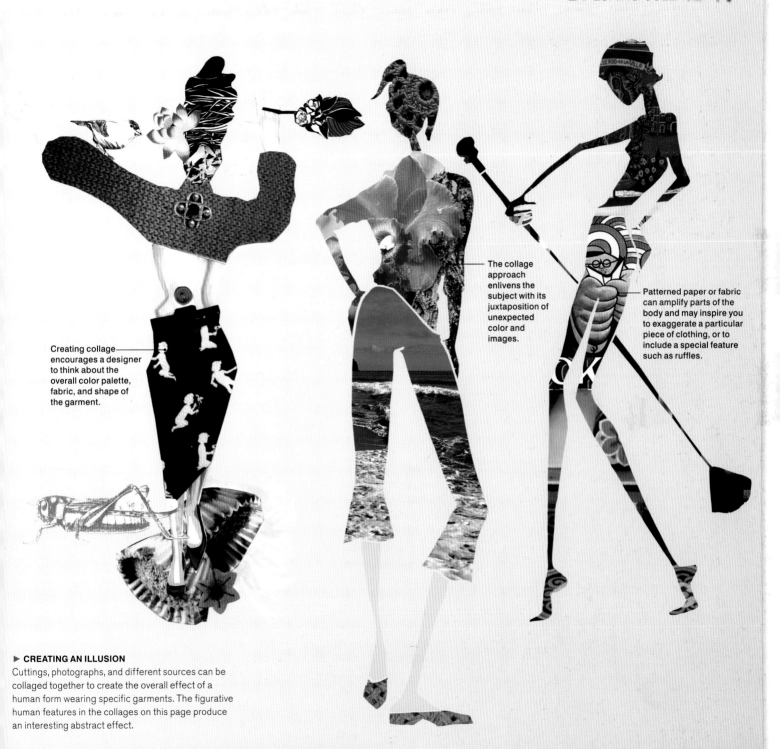

Creating collage encourages a designer to think about the overall color palette, fabric, and shape of the garment.

The collage approach enlivens the subject with its juxtaposition of unexpected color and images.

Patterned paper or fabric can amplify parts of the body and may inspire you to exaggerate a particular piece of clothing, or to include a special feature such as ruffles.

▶ **CREATING AN ILLUSION**
Cuttings, photographs, and different sources can be collaged together to create the overall effect of a human form wearing specific garments. The figurative human features in the collages on this page produce an interesting abstract effect.

UNIT 13 Not just pencil

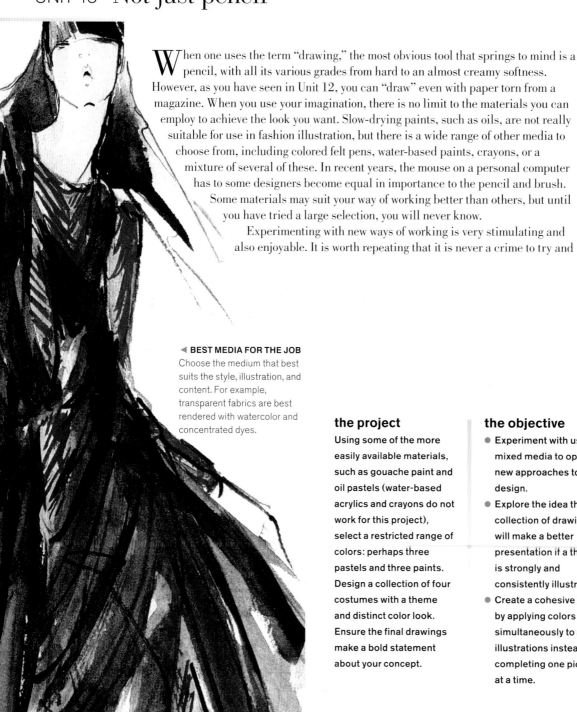

When one uses the term "drawing," the most obvious tool that springs to mind is a pencil, with all its various grades from hard to an almost creamy softness. However, as you have seen in Unit 12, you can "draw" even with paper torn from a magazine. When you use your imagination, there is no limit to the materials you can employ to achieve the look you want. Slow-drying paints, such as oils, are not really suitable for use in fashion illustration, but there is a wide range of other media to choose from, including colored felt pens, water-based paints, crayons, or a mixture of several of these. In recent years, the mouse on a personal computer has to some designers become equal in importance to the pencil and brush. Some materials may suit your way of working better than others, but until you have tried a large selection, you will never know.

Experimenting with new ways of working is very stimulating and also enjoyable. It is worth repeating that it is never a crime to try and

◀ **BEST MEDIA FOR THE JOB**
Choose the medium that best suits the style, illustration, and content. For example, transparent fabrics are best rendered with watercolor and concentrated dyes.

SELF-CRITIQUE
● Did you choose colors that work well together?
● Were your final illustrations bold?
● Did they have a cohesive look portraying the essence of your designs?
● Was full use made of your different materials?

SEE ALSO
● Illustrating bold print, p. 86
● Learn to love your roughs, p. 94
● Planning a range, p. 98

the project
Using some of the more easily available materials, such as gouache paint and oil pastels (water-based acrylics and crayons do not work for this project), select a restricted range of colors: perhaps three pastels and three paints. Design a collection of four costumes with a theme and distinct color look. Ensure the final drawings make a bold statement about your concept.

the objective
● Experiment with using mixed media to open up new approaches to a design.
● Explore the idea that a collection of drawings will make a better presentation if a theme is strongly and consistently illustrated.
● Create a cohesive look by applying colors simultaneously to all illustrations instead of completing one picture at a time.

the process
From the vast range of inspiration toward which you were directed earlier in this book, select a theme on which to base your collection. Try out your chosen colors together to make sure they are a good combination. Next, test some ideas by first drawing with oil pastels, then washing over the marks with watery but full-colored paint. The oil pastel will resist the paint and create interesting contrasts.

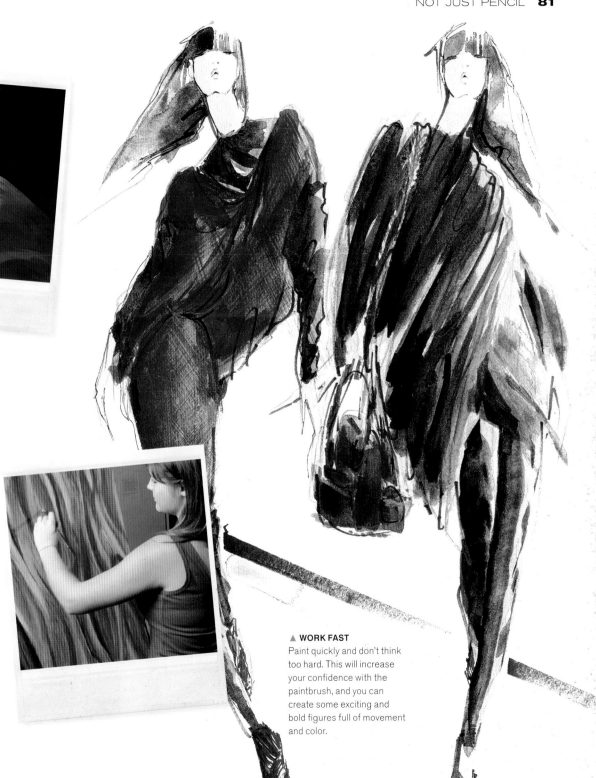

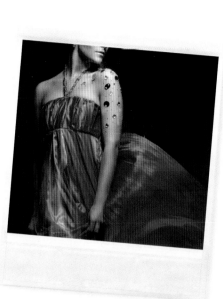

▲ **GATHERING INSPIRATION**
Take photographs of different fabrics draped on models. Use these images as a guide when drawing the shapes and lines of your illustrations.

Then lay out four sheets of paper (20 x 30 in. /50 x 75 cm) in front of you. Using pencil, and covering as much of the page as possible, confidently draw the outlines of your designs.

Now methodically apply the oil pastels, color by color, to all the drawings simultaneously. Keep your nerve! Finally, use the paint, applying one color at a time to all the illustrations.

▲ **WORK FAST**
Paint quickly and don't think too hard. This will increase your confidence with the paintbrush, and you can create some exciting and bold figures full of movement and color.

UNIT 13 Not just pencil

fail. It is understandable to want to have pride in your work, but you will produce only mediocre ideas if you always play it safe.

Experimenting with applying and mixing different media can achieve stunning results. Unusual combinations of techniques lend a freshness and originality to fashion illustrations that make them stand out. A glowing effect can be achieved by using pastels and a watercolor wash. When both media are utilized to their maximum effect, the illustrations seem to "pop" off the page. By choosing color palettes before the design is committed to paper, and then applying the colors step by step onto the whole series of illustrations at once, the common concept of the design comes through strongly. Working in this way, all the pictures will come to completion at the same time, and a powerful overall look will emerge.

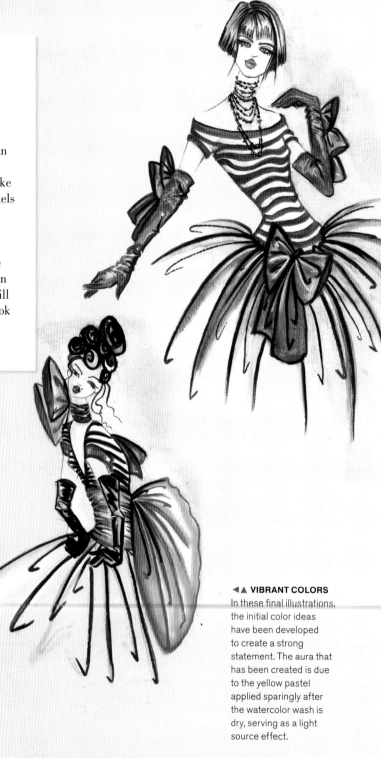

◄▲ VIBRANT COLORS
In these final illustrations, the initial color ideas have been developed to create a strong statement. The aura that has been created is due to the yellow pastel applied sparingly after the watercolor wash is dry, serving as a light source effect.

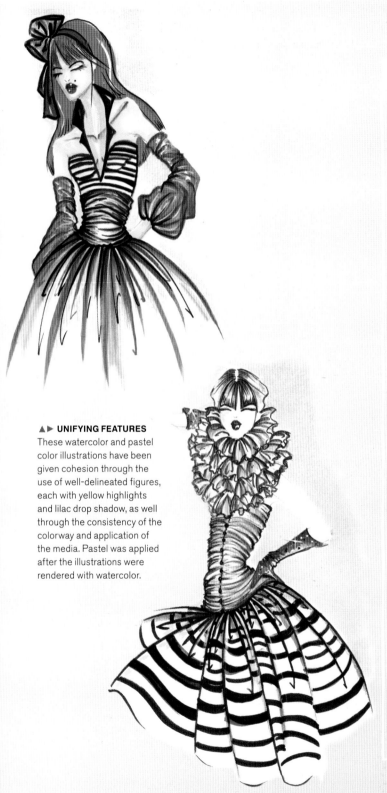

Fantasy theme

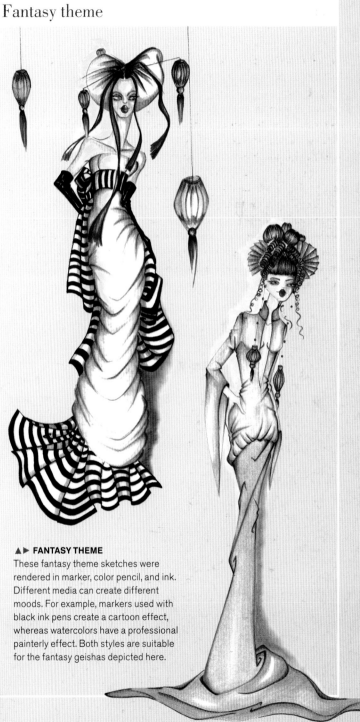

▲▶ UNIFYING FEATURES
These watercolor and pastel color illustrations have been given cohesion through the use of well-delineated figures, each with yellow highlights and lilac drop shadow, as well through the consistency of the colorway and application of the media. Pastel was applied after the illustrations were rendered with watercolor.

▲▶ FANTASY THEME
These fantasy theme sketches were rendered in marker, color pencil, and ink. Different media can create different moods. For example, markers used with black ink pens create a cartoon effect, whereas watercolors have a professional painterly effect. Both styles are suitable for the fantasy geishas depicted here.

inspiration file

Laying out your page

A designer is in the business of visual communication, whether the information is presented purely pictorially or with the addition of words. The pages of this book have been designed to impart the information of text and illustration with maximum clarity and visual impact. That is what you should aspire to in any work that is to sell your ideas successfully to the client.

* Ask yourself what the main focus of your page should be.

* Think about scale before you start. Make sure that you fill the page with your main point of interest. Don't add other details that are unnecessary.

* Try to use an effective pose for displaying your chosen item.

Start out by confidently drawing a dynamic image that fills the page for maximum impact. Do not leave too much negative space around the drawing. It is important that your drawings reflect the spirit of the subject. If, for example, you are illustrating accessories that require a focal point, the drawing should be equally focused on the particular item, as in the sketch of the handbag designs, opposite. It is worth making rough sketches to plan your page and designs, ensuring the information you wish to portray is foremost. For example, drawing elongated legs when the point of interest is an accessory wastes valuable page space and is compositionally inefficient.

It is worth remembering that clutter can also be a distraction. Sometimes less is really more. Focus on the main message you are trying to portray. It can be helpful

sometimes to prepare a rough page with a watercolor wash or broad, loose marker sketch. One technique to ensure you fill the page is to try thinking outside the page edges. You can achieve this by pairing the sheet of paper you're working with onto a larger sheet, then drawing over the edges. This will allow you to scale the drawing to the appropriate size. The same effect can be achieved by starting on a sheet of paper larger than you intend to display, completing your illustration, and then cropping it to produce the best composition.

When planning a page layout, it is best to start at the top and plot where you want the head. Then work down the page to the bottom, plotting the figure, and staying aware of the side perimeters. You should strive to achieve balance in the overall composition and page layout. Balance doesn't necessarily mean uniform or symmetrical, just a visual without any one thing sticking out or feeling out of place. The compositional success should also reflect the garment as the primary focus.

In fashion illustration, you will mainly be working in portrait format, in which the sheet is positioned vertically, as opposed to landscape, which is horizontally longer. This general rule is due to the longer vertical nature of the majority of illustrations. However, as we have seen throughout this book, rules are meant to be broken, once you know them. As you see, this book is in square format, which produces a landscape spread across two pages.

◀ **USE YOUR SKETCHBOOK**
Use your sketchbook to experiment with filling a page. On your final layout, you should try to make a strong statement about whatever you are drawing, avoiding unnecessary clutter, so work out your ideas in a sketchbook first.

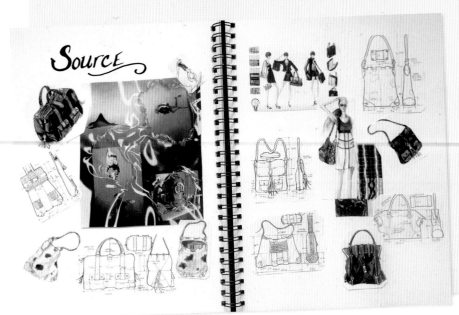

Source

▶ **DOUBLE VISION**
Using more than one figure in the same illustration can strengthen the impact of the garment—but be careful not to lose your focus.

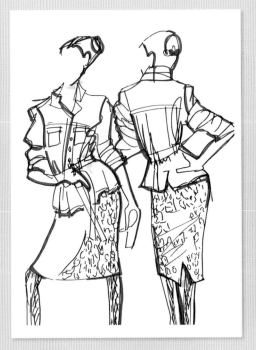

▶ **BALANCED STANCE**
This dramatic pose is most effective for showing off sportswear, especially sports pants. Pant details, such as the cut, bottom leg shape, and knee pads, can be conveyed well in this exuberant pose.

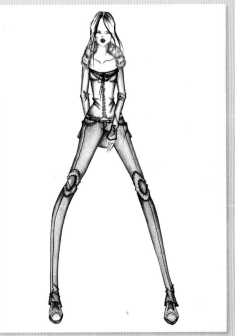

▶ **MIXING IT UP**
Try using figures in different poses to keep things fresh in your layouts. If using a busy scheme, make sure it is balanced by sticking to a limited color palette.

▶ **KEEP IT SIMPLE**
When the illustration is highlighting accessory items (as seen far right), it is best to keep the accompanying garments simple. A cropped figure can direct the focus toward the intended item.

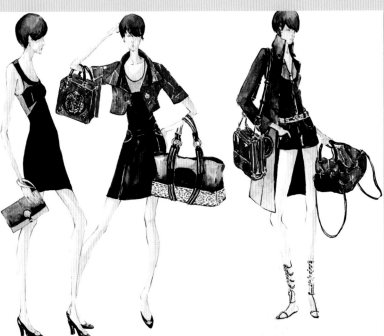

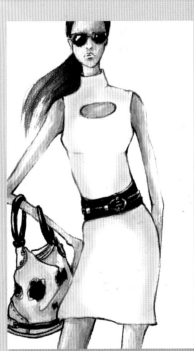

UNIT 14 Illustrating bold print

A good designer is a good communicator. In order to communicate design, the skills and objectivity of an illustrator are essential. A good illustrator is able to communicate ideas effectively on paper. A good designer, therefore, is a good illustrator.

Illustrating the work of other designers requires the same skill as portraying your own work. Although fashion illustrators will of course bring their own design skills to the interpretation of garments, they have been commissioned to depict.

In this unit, you will look at illustrating prints and motifs on garments in order to practice the process of observing clothes closely,

then capturing their story on paper. You will learn how to use the page effectively, how to employ both digital and traditional media to imitate striking designs, and how to make a strong statement about design ideas.

Boldness is always the best policy for realizing a design drawing. Subtle designs are more difficult to render because the minor nuances can easily be lost. An uncompromising "between the eyes" statement produces striking results, whether it involves a strong silhouette, vibrant colors, or a combination of both. The bright patterns of the Pucci dresses illustrated here provide a great starting

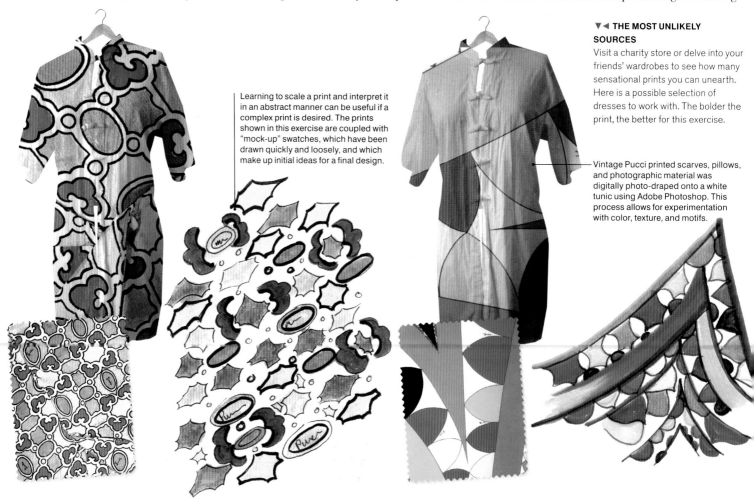

Learning to scale a print and interpret it in an abstract manner can be useful if a complex print is desired. The prints shown in this exercise are coupled with "mock-up" swatches, which have been drawn quickly and loosely, and which make up initial ideas for a final design.

▼◄ **THE MOST UNLIKELY SOURCES**
Visit a charity store or delve into your friends' wardrobes to see how many sensational prints you can unearth. Here is a possible selection of dresses to work with. The bolder the print, the better for this exercise.

Vintage Pucci printed scarves, pillows, and photographic material was digitally photo-draped onto a white tunic using Adobe Photoshop. This process allows for experimentation with color, texture, and motifs.

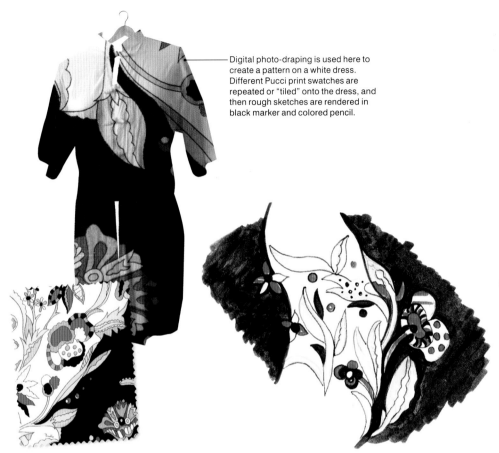

Digital photo-draping is used here to create a pattern on a white dress. Different Pucci print swatches are repeated or "tiled" onto the dress, and then rough sketches are rendered in black marker and colored pencil.

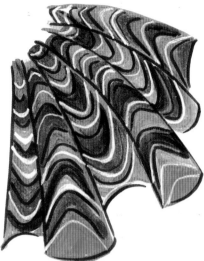

◄▲ MIX AND MATCH
Explore ways of matching colors and motifs, infusing marker with pencil for instance. Mix and blend the markers or ink pens with colored pencils to achieve the bright colors desired. Practice shorthand sketching ideas for conveying assorted motifs. These rough shorthand renderings could be lateral or impressionistic, as demonstrated in the rough try-out versions shown here.

the project
Research images of Pucci dresses, garments, or bright vintage prints. Complete at least four bold illustrations using any medium you think appropriate. This theme could especially suit markers and pen, or perhaps bright inks and watercolors.

the objective
● Observe closely the garments you choose to draw.

● Work out a shorthand way of drawing the print.
● Find a suitable pose that fills the page and makes a strong statement.

the process
Research some striking prints by taking photographs of displays in stores or by collecting images from magazines and web sites. You will have the color and design references on hand, so this is not a creative exercise but an assignment geared

toward acquiring technical skills. You will be discovering ways to recreate color and forms faithfully. Try to reproduce the colors exactly, and explore different ways of representing the motifs. Sketch out your illustrations with poses that both fill the page and highlight the print.

Lightly draw preliminary outlines in colored pencil; start working in the main colors, marking the body and construction details

such as sleeves and neckline. Complete your four drawings by adding figure details: hair, face, and accessories, if desired.

SEE ALSO
● Digital fabric and colorways, p. 114
● Color palettes, p. 118

SELF-CRITIQUE
● Are the prints in your garment illustrations distinguishable?
● How well are the colors matched to the original garment?
● Do your motifs look like the original?
● Is the print scale correct?
● Did you choose a suitable medium?

UNIT 14 Illustrating bold print

point for demonstrating how to represent motifs vibrantly and make best use of the entire page layout. Pucci garments are timeless, and there will be many interpretations available for you to choose from.

Today's print designers have many options available when producing vibrant prints. They often use computers to enhance or entirely render prints for production purposes. In these examples, we use the application Adobe Photoshop to rough out and storyboard the original Pucci idea in a technique known as digital photo-draping or "tiling." Then, we faithfully render the salient aspects of the Pucci prints in marker and prisma color pencil.

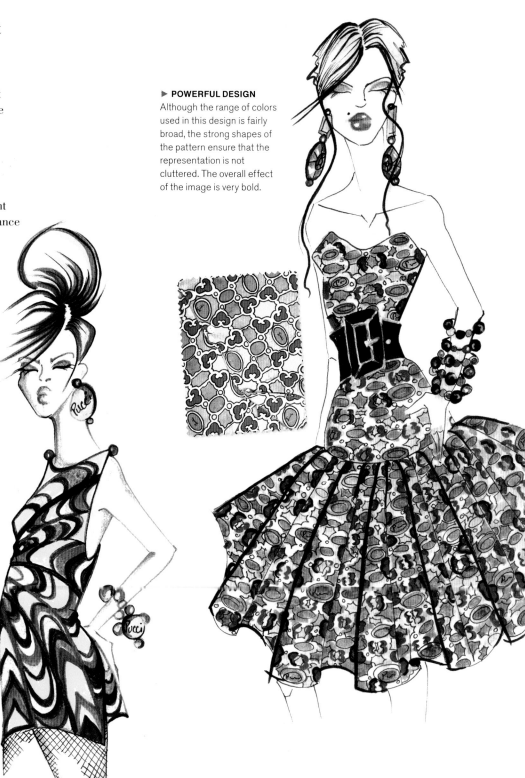

▶ **POWERFUL DESIGN**
Although the range of colors used in this design is fairly broad, the strong shapes of the pattern ensure that the representation is not cluttered. The overall effect of the image is very bold.

▶ **AN ALTERNATIVE VIEW**
Because the focal point of the designs is the print and not the garment, the decision was made to draw from the side, a point of view sometimes neglected when illustrating fashion design.

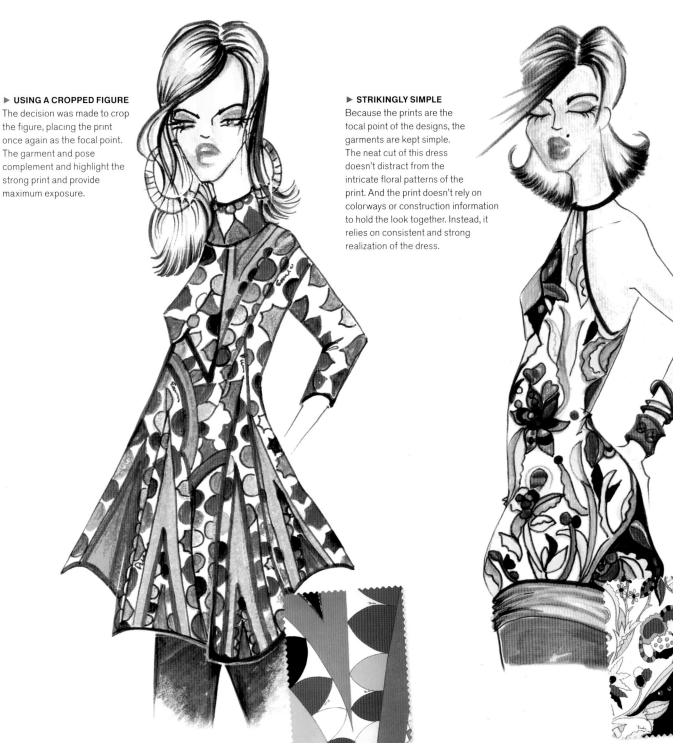

▶ **USING A CROPPED FIGURE**
The decision was made to crop the figure, placing the print once again as the focal point. The garment and pose complement and highlight the strong print and provide maximum exposure.

▶ **STRIKINGLY SIMPLE**
Because the prints are the focal point of the designs, the garments are kept simple. The neat cut of this dress doesn't distract from the intricate floral patterns of the print. And the print doesn't rely on colorways or construction information to hold the look together. Instead, it relies on consistent and strong realization of the dress.

3 Planning and designing

As a designer, you cannot afford to be self-indulgent, but should instead try to produce work that is commercially viable. This chapter explains how to develop a cohesive collection and plan your range to offer as much choice as possible. You will also learn how to target your designs toward a customer profile and specific end use, and to work within the constraints of the season and budget. The chapter also examines how to apply a color palette effectively throughout a collection and how to structure fabric to create the silhouettes you want.

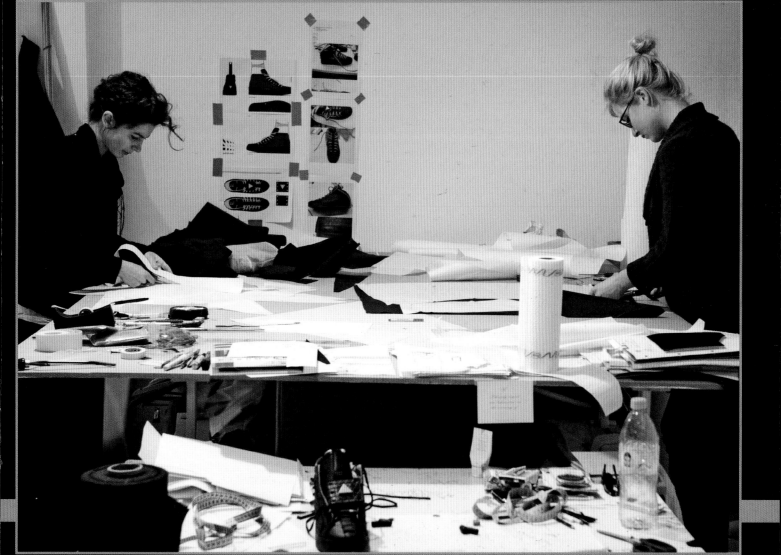

* Working with a scrapbook can help you to develop cohesion—you can naturally combine your sketches with inspiring magazine cuttings.

* Remember that initial sketches don't need to be perfectly drawn. Try to treat your roughs purely as a means to developing ideas.

Creating a cohesive collection

Fashion designers develop a whole range of related ideas to produce groups of garments that work not only as stand-alone outfits but also as a collection. A consistent approach to important factors such as color, shape, pattern, and proportion helps to create this cohesion.

It is this systematic development of ideas that enables the designer to think laterally and to get the most out of each concept. With practice and experience, you will learn not to settle for the first idea that comes along but to push yourself to generate a series of related concepts. You may be surprised at the results as you progress away from your starting point and down new avenues of creativity. The collections that you develop will have a natural cohesion because they contain similar and related themes, and you will soon find yourself creating a coordinated range of garments rather than separate and unrelated outfits.

An important factor in this process is to learn to be comfortable with thinking out loud on paper. This means feeling relaxed about noting down your ideas and sketching out a series of designs. You must learn to love your roughs! A blank page can be intimidating, and it is easy for the novice designer to become so concerned with the appearance of the initial sketches that the actual design process takes second place. With practice, you will gain confidence and be more relaxed about encouraging the flow of ideas. Remember that you are just developing your thoughts, not trying to create a masterpiece. It does not matter how well executed these roughs are; they are for your purposes only and do not need to be judged by anyone else. All that matters is that the roughs assist you in working through your stream of

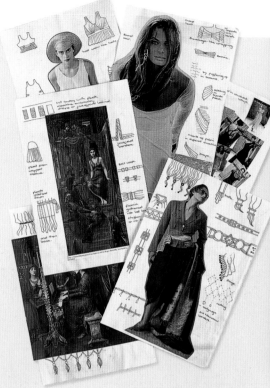

▲ **DRAWING ON THE IDEAS BANK**
Store garment-detailing ideas in your sketchbook and select themes to apply to a group of garments in order to achieve a naturally cohesive collection.

▼ **WORKING WITH "FLATS"**
Working with flat garment outlines may help you develop related ideas and build up a unified collection.

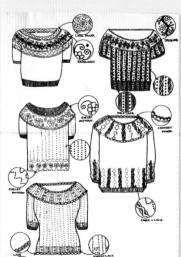

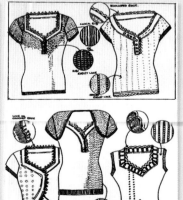

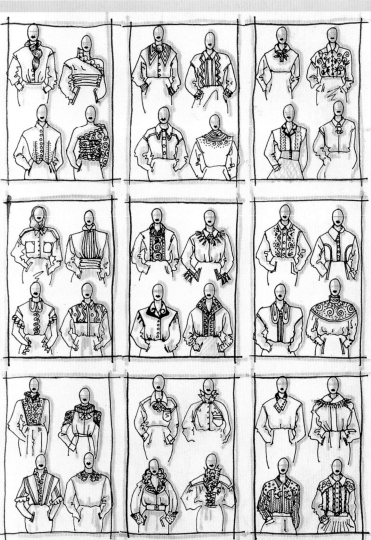

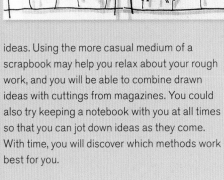

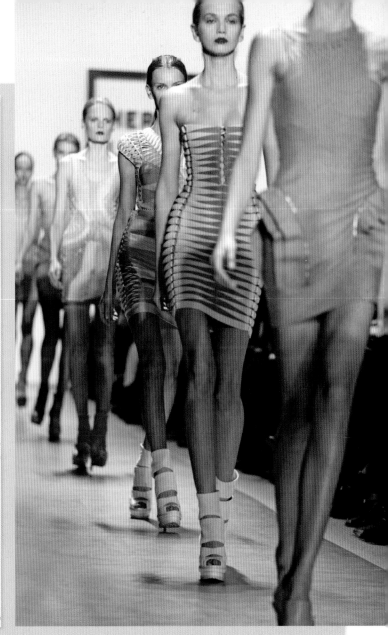

ideas. Using the more casual medium of a scrapbook may help you relax about your rough work, and you will be able to combine drawn ideas with cuttings from magazines. You could also try keeping a notebook with you at all times so that you can jot down ideas as they come. With time, you will discover which methods work best for you.

▲ THINKING OUT LOUD ON PAPER
This page of sketches is an example of planning on paper. Don't worry if your initial drawings are quickly executed and very rough.

▲ MIX AND MATCH
This collection by Betty Jackson comprises a selection of different garments, including eveningwear, daywear, and outerwear, and demonstrates how designers need to plan coordinated ranges with a unifying overall look.

UNIT 15 Learn to love your roughs

It's time to start thinking like a designer! The more you can relax and not worry about how someone else might respond to your drawings, the better they will be. Remember that you are not yet producing final illustrations or even communicating your ideas to anyone else. You are simply thinking out loud on paper. If you feel daunted by the blank page, try beginning by jotting down a list of words as ideas come into your head. You might include descriptions such as "rounded," "sophisticated," "feminine," or "soft" to evoke your target customer and the kinds of garments that you might design for her or him. This will make starting to sketch much less intimidating. Your rough sketches may be drawn on a figure or as flat garments with carefully considered proportions.

The creation of roughs is an important part of the design process, especially if the designer is trying to give the collection a strong overall look. Roughs are

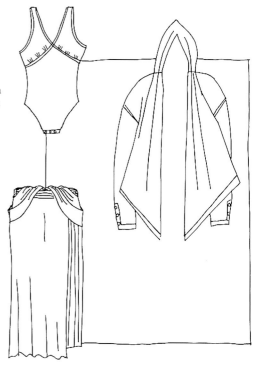

► A VARIETY OF SHAPES
Initially, you could explore a number of garment shapes using "flats." Remember that you are aiming to produce a collection of outfits comprising related but varied garment types.

the project

Choose your theme and produce some first rough garment ideas, considering in particular what it is that inspires you about your research. Select the strongest ideas and expand on these, using a layout pad. Trace over your initial visual thoughts to produce a series of designs, changing one element with each new drawing. The result will be a series of variations on a theme.

the objective

● Create a set of ideas that holds together as a collection.
● Use roughs to expand on your starting point.
● Avoid the obvious and develop your own unique style.
● Assess your ideas as you work and develop the strongest designs.

the process

Think carefully about your starting point, considering its colors, textures, shapes, patterns, and symbolism. Jot down some ideas on paper, using words as well as quick sketches. Taking the stronger ideas further, produce some rough designs on a layout pad. The thinner paper of the layout pad will allow designs to be easily traced, one on top of the other, but take care not to work into the paper too heavily, since it can bleed color through to the sketch below. Work by tearing out one drawing and laying it beneath a clean page to make the next, adapting the previous design. Push yourself to produce lots of ideas, changing one element with each new drawing and building up step by step a series of related garments. Now you are truly thinking like a designer, as you create a cohesive collection.

Aim to produce about twenty rough outfit ideas. As you work, keep in mind the inspiring features of the starting point. Assess all the rough drawings by placing them next to each other (you can photocopy your sketchbook pages and line them up, if necessary). Select the five strongest ideas for your portfolio—those that best capture your inspiration and hold together as a collection. These drawings can then be perfected to create finished illustrations.

SEE ALSO
● Planning a range, p. 98
● Customer focus, p. 104
● Working drawings, p. 130

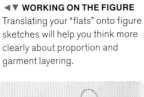

WORKING ON THE FIGURE
Translating your "flats" onto figure sketches will help you think more clearly about proportion and garment layering.

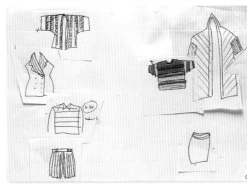

LAYERING SKETCHES
Work with a layout pad, drawing garments either on the figure or, as shown here, as flat sketches. Tracing ideas, one on top of the other, encourages a progression of ideas while ensuring that garment outlines remain related.

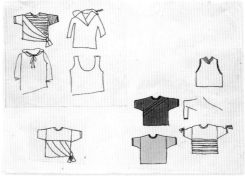

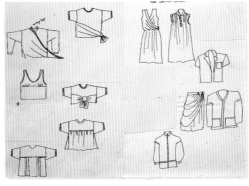

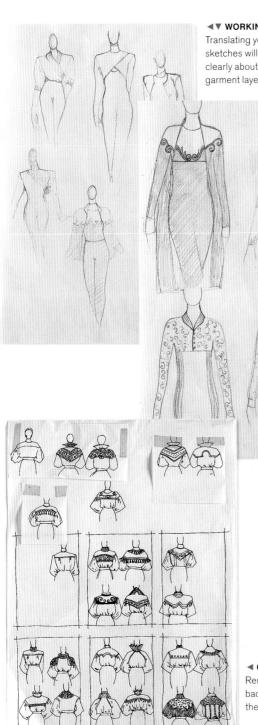

CONSIDERING ALL THE ANGLES
Remember to work through ideas for back views as well as to think about the front of your designs.

SELF-CRITIQUE
- Were you confident enough to note down your ideas in a non-timid way?
- Did you expand from your starting point to create unique designs rather than simply drawing the obvious?
- Have you chosen the strongest ideas from your roughs?
- Do your five chosen roughs look as if they belong together?

UNIT 15 Learn to love your roughs

used to get all the related ideas about a source down on paper. Only once this has been done is it possible to assess all the sketches objectively and decide which work best as a collection and should therefore be taken to the next stage. As shown here, the successful roughs are those that work as individual pieces but also sit well with the other ideas because they have certain design themes in common.

The designs pictured here are clearly related to one another in both the details and the sihouette, yet are interesting and unique garments in themselves. Refining ideas beyond the rough stage ensures that designs progress beyond the obvious and prevents the collection from being derivative or repetitious.

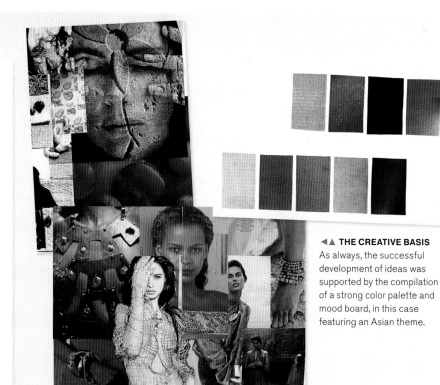

◄▲ THE CREATIVE BASIS
As always, the successful development of ideas was supported by the compilation of a strong color palette and mood board, in this case featuring an Asian theme.

◄ FIRST THOUGHTS
This rough was used to establish silhouette and proportion; the decorative detail was added later in the process.

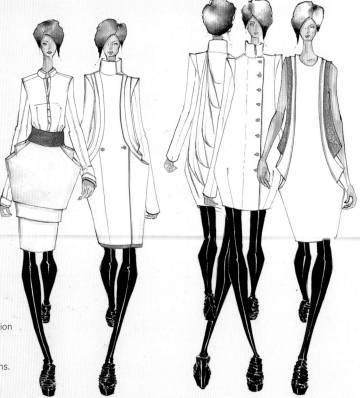

► FINALIZING IDEAS
These final illustrations reflect Westernized fashion shapes while retaining subtle references to the Asian theme of the roughs.

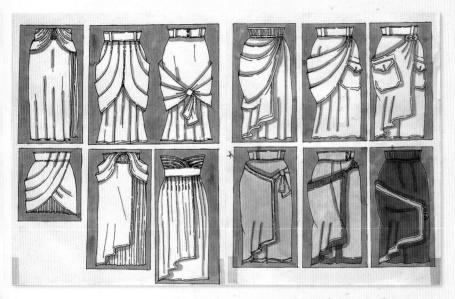

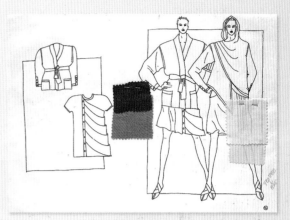

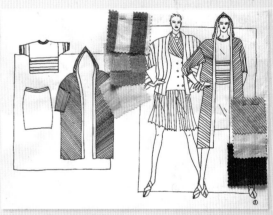

▲ **OFFERING VARIETY**
An idea such as draping soft fabric
can be applied in many different
ways to similar garment shapes.

▼ **THEMES IN COMMON**
In these roughs, the garments
already have the feel of a
cohesive collection, unified by
an Asian look and design
themes such as the fringing
and embellished details.

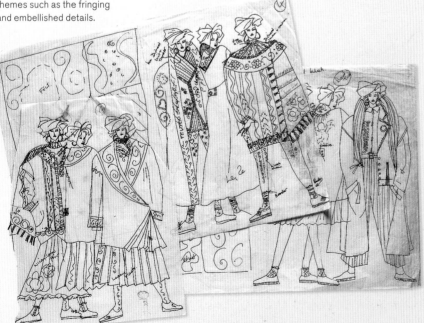

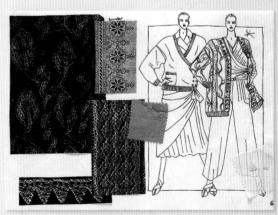

▲ **PATTERN, COLOR, AND SILHOUETTE**
These illustrations have been given a unified
feel by the pattern and color of the fabric
and by the flared silhouettes of the designs.

UNIT 16 Planning a range

The words "range" and "collection" are often used interchangeably in the fashion industry to denote the group of garments created each season by a designer. However, "range" also has more specifically commercial overtones. Range planning involves considering your designs in terms of a complete wardrobe of coordinated garments, incorporating a balance of tops, bottoms, dresses, outerwear, and so on. When you see garments by your favorite designer displayed in a boutique, you are experiencing range planning. The newness and trendiness of the garments are obviously important, but the boutique also needs to appeal to its customers with a variety of options of garment type that coordinate and are interchangeable.

Sometimes a client will brief a designer to create a specific range. This might be a swimwear, bridal, or eveningwear collection, for example, and the choice of items to include in the range will be very much dictated by the brief. If you have been asked to design an eveningwear range, you will probably want to

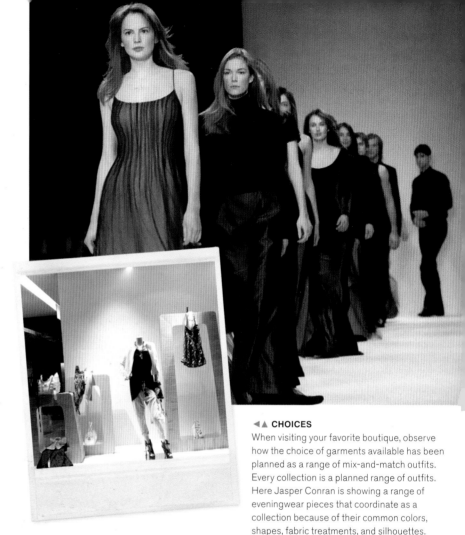

◄▲ **CHOICES**
When visiting your favorite boutique, observe how the choice of garments available has been planned as a range of mix-and-match outfits. Every collection is a planned range of outfits. Here Jasper Conran is showing a range of eveningwear pieces that coordinate as a collection because of their common colors, shapes, fabric treatments, and silhouettes.

the project
First brainstorm ideas about a daywear range, without worrying too much about the appearance of your sketches. Then map out garments that you think might be suitable for inclusion in the range and consider how they can be worn together as outfits. Finally, illustrate the best combinations as finished drawings of eight outfits.

the objective
- Select designs that hang together as a collection.
- Offer a good choice of individual pieces within the collection.
- Create a range of garments that look good in their own right but can be easily mixed and matched to make different outfits.

the process
You should be gaining confidence in your rough sketches as you work through the projects in this book. Again, just rough out the ideas as they come to you and do not worry too much about what the sketches look like—you do not have to show them to anybody else. There is no strict plan at this stage, simply an outpouring of thought about garments that might constitute a daywear range.

Reconsider your raw ideas, as you have done in previous projects, this time exploring how they could work together as a range. Try to include a good selection of separates, such as short and long skirts, trousers, dresses, tops, outerwear, and so on. The garments should coordinate and be interchangeable so that they can work both as a range and as individual pieces. As you plan, use quick sketches as an aide-mémoire, or even draw up a grid in your notebook and list possible combinations of garments. Then, bearing in mind the points above, select the designs that you want to include in your range. Finally, draw finished illustrations of eight outfits.

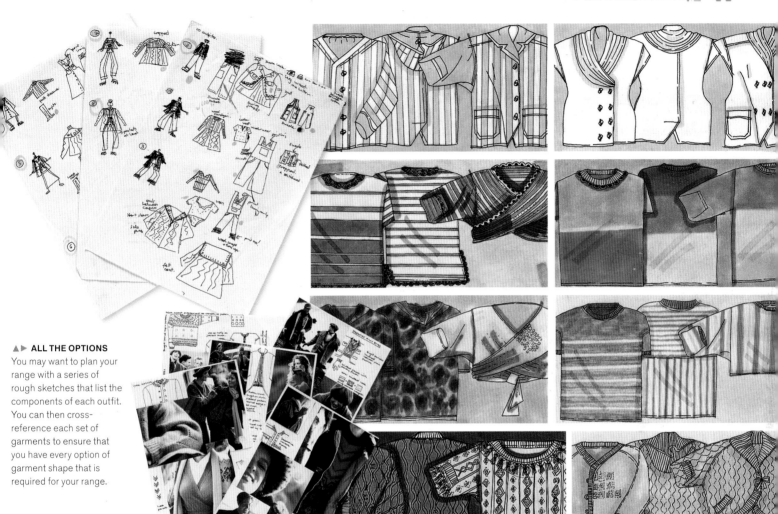

▲▶ ALL THE OPTIONS
You may want to plan your range with a series of rough sketches that list the components of each outfit. You can then cross-reference each set of garments to ensure that you have every option of garment shape that is required for your range.

▲▶ CONSIDERING THE DETAILS
Think carefully about the construction and finishing of each piece to ensure that you offer maximum choice within your range.

SELF-CRITIQUE
- Have you created a cohesive collection of garments?
- Do all the pieces work well together throughout the range (and not just as part of the outfits that you have illustrated)?
- Would a customer of a boutique selling your designs have a good choice of garment types?

SEE ALSO
- Creating a cohesive collection, p. 92
- Learn to love your roughs, p. 94
- Occasions, seasons, budgets, p. 108

UNIT 16 Planning a range

include a large number of dresses—as in collections of eveningwear by Versace. It is perfectly acceptable to bias your range to one garment type, so long as the decision is based on the client's brief.

The goal of range planning should be to tempt customers into buying as many items as possible—this is more complicated than it appears. An early fall contemporary career-wear collection, such as the one featured here, will require a variety of pieces that can be interchangeably worn together or worn as separates. The range illustrated here offers a good selection of garments that clearly coordinate while avoiding unnecessary duplication.

The age group of a target customer will also affect the design, fabric, and construction. The planned range here is targeted toward the trendier career-oriented customer, but could be adapted for a more contemporary budget-conscious consumer.

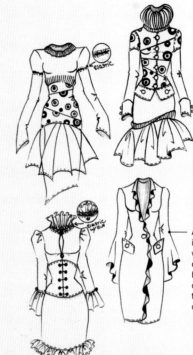

◀ ▼ **COORDINATION IS KEY**
Every collection is divided into groups or ranges. Three, four, or five groups compose a collection. Every designer and manufacturer decides on what the predominant feature in the range is.

A career wardrobe might include jackets and skirts within a range or group of designs. However, it would still be necessary to offer a choice of other pieces to appeal to the target customer and provide coordinating separates.

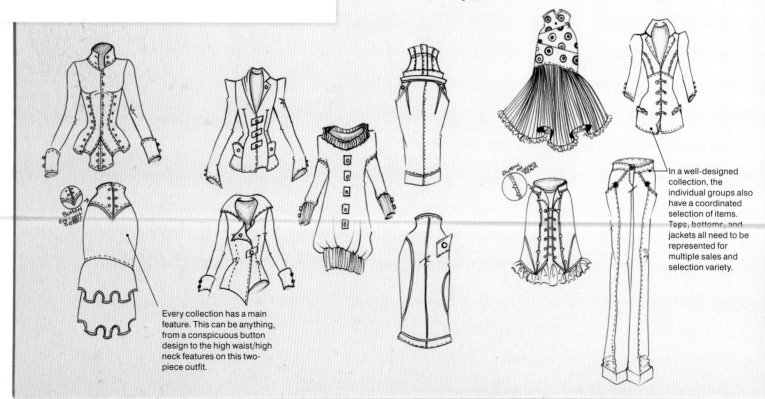

Every collection has a main feature. This can be anything, from a conspicuous button design to the high waist/high neck features on this two-piece outfit.

In a well-designed collection, the individual groups also have a coordinated selection of items. Tops, bottoms, and jackets all need to be represented for multiple sales and selection variety.

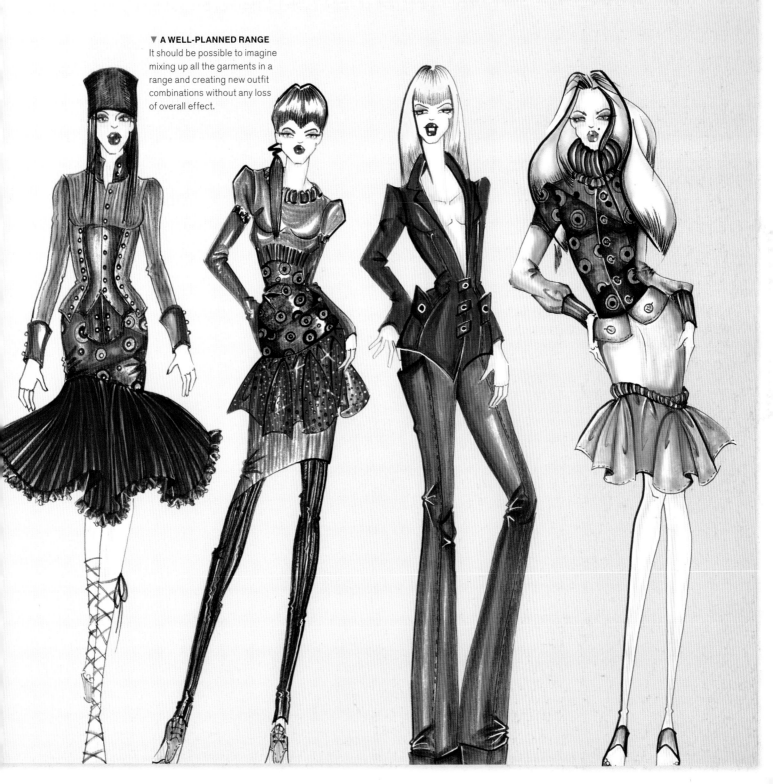

▼ **A WELL-PLANNED RANGE**
It should be possible to imagine mixing up all the garments in a range and creating new outfit combinations without any loss of overall effect.

inspiration file

Designing to a brief

As a fashion designer, you will always have a client or target customer in mind. You cannot afford to be self-indulgent and simply create designs to suit your own tastes. You will notice that all the famous fashion houses have their own particular styles that reflect the philosophy of the designer.

There are various limitations associated with working to a design brief, and it is best to confirm them before you begin. Your budget, for example, will be dictated by the price at which your garments can be sold. It is common in the fashion industry to establish a rigid and logical price structure for all the pieces in a collection—a vest top will be cheaper than a long-sleeved garment, for example—and your designs should reflect this. A garment that is very embellished will have a high perceived value, but the designer must be certain that the customer is willing to pay the increased price.

You also need to be sure you are designing appropriate garments for the time of year that they will appear, and that your work is in line with fashion trend predictions for that season.

Another very important factor is the nature of your target customer. You should aim to construct a profile of the kind of person who is likely to wear the designs you will produce for each project. Fashion designers call this imaginary, or indeed sometimes real, person their "muse." You can create your own muse by building up a selection of magazine images that represent your customer. You will need to

▶ **NICHE MARKETS**
It is important to have the ability to design outside of your comfort zone or specialization. Many niche markets, such as the plus size clothing market, offer opportunities for the budding designer.

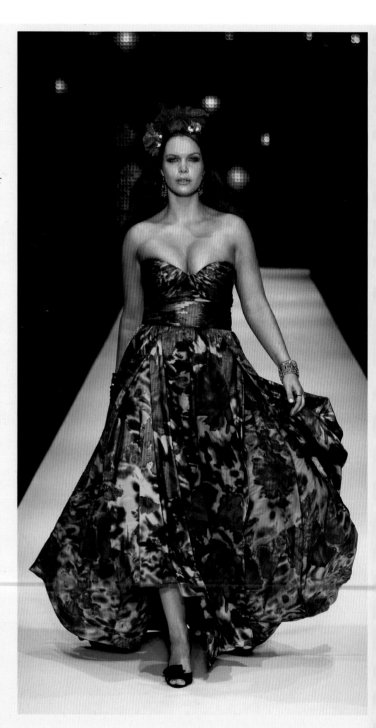

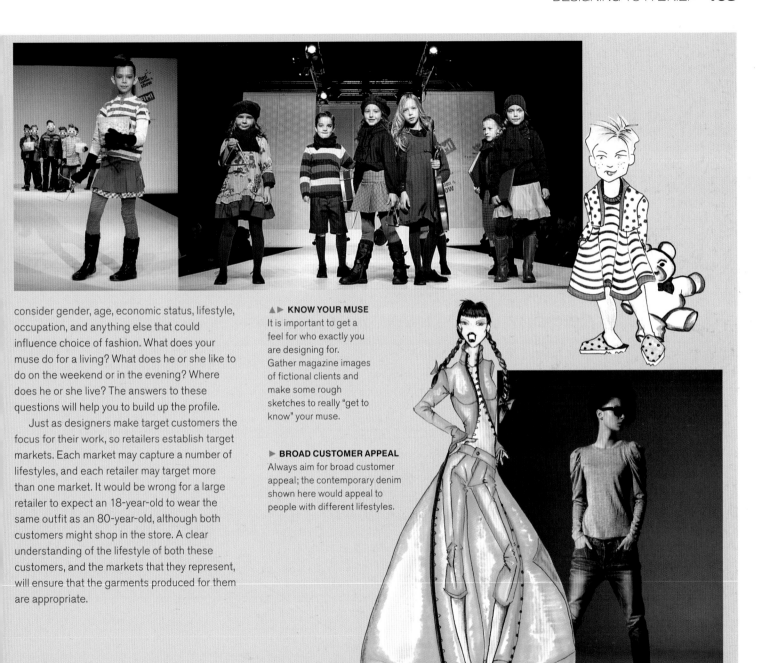

consider gender, age, economic status, lifestyle, occupation, and anything else that could influence choice of fashion. What does your muse do for a living? What does he or she like to do on the weekend or in the evening? Where does he or she live? The answers to these questions will help you to build up the profile.

Just as designers make target customers the focus for their work, so retailers establish target markets. Each market may capture a number of lifestyles, and each retailer may target more than one market. It would be wrong for a large retailer to expect an 18-year-old to wear the same outfit as an 80-year-old, although both customers might shop in the store. A clear understanding of the lifestyle of both these customers, and the markets that they represent, will ensure that the garments produced for them are appropriate.

▲ ▶ **KNOW YOUR MUSE**
It is important to get a feel for who exactly you are designing for. Gather magazine images of fictional clients and make some rough sketches to really "get to know" your muse.

▶ **BROAD CUSTOMER APPEAL**
Always aim for broad customer appeal; the contemporary denim shown here would appeal to people with different lifestyles.

UNIT 17 Customer focus

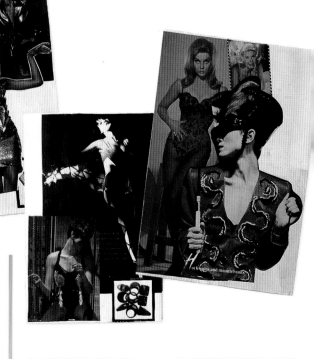

As a fashion designer, you need to develop the ability to work with enthusiasm and passion on projects that might not appeal to you personally. It is not enough to want to create only the designs that you like. The fashion designer differs from the artist in that there will usually be a customer or client in mind, who will ultimately be paying for the

the project

Pick an advertisement from a current fashion magazine that features a person who looks interesting. The advertisement will suggest a lifestyle associated with the person depicted. You have just met your latest customer! In this unit, you will design a collection of eight finished outfits targeted at this person. Challenge yourself by choosing someone very different from the people you have designed for in the past.

the objective

- Learn to research your customer's lifestyle.
- Target your collection.
- Practice the ability to work outside your personal preferences.
- Add a project with a very different flavor to your portfolio.

the process

Look through some of your fashion magazines and find an image of an interesting person. Try to go for someone for whom you would not normally consider designing: a person from a different gender or age group, for example. Advertisements are good to work with because they usually suggest a lifestyle associated with the people featured.

Start by jotting down words that describe your chosen customer. How old is he or she? Where does he or she live, work, and go on vacation? How wealthy is this person? What sort of car does your customer drive, and which newspaper does he or she read? Where is your customer likely to wear the clothes that you are designing? Gradually build up a complete lifestyle profile of your new customer.

Next you can start to plan your range, aiming ultimately to produce eight finished outfits. As you do this, consider your customer's lifestyle, where the clothes will be worn, and how expensive they are likely to be. Put together a color palette, isolating no more than six to eight colors that you can see within your chosen magazine image. Finally, draw your eight finished outfits, remembering that they are not intended to please you but to appeal to your customer. Endeavor to maintain both enthusiasm and professional pride in your work, even though it might not be to your own taste.

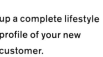

▲ **DARE TO EXPERIMENT**
When choosing the image of your potential customer, challenge yourself to select someone who would wear garments that are very different from your previous designs.

SEE ALSO
- Designing to a brief, p. 102
- Occasions, seasons, budgets, p. 108

SELF-CRITIQUE
- Did you truly challenge yourself with your choice of customer?
- Have you been able to work beyond merely designing garments that you like?
- Did you maintain your enthusiasm while working on styles that come less naturally to you?
- Are you satisfied that you have produced an interesting design outcome?

▼ ▶ APPROPRIATE IDEAS
The outlines and fabrics used in these designs are consistently targeted at a customer with more conservative tastes. Keep referring to your lifestyle research: are your ideas truly appropriate to your customer's needs?

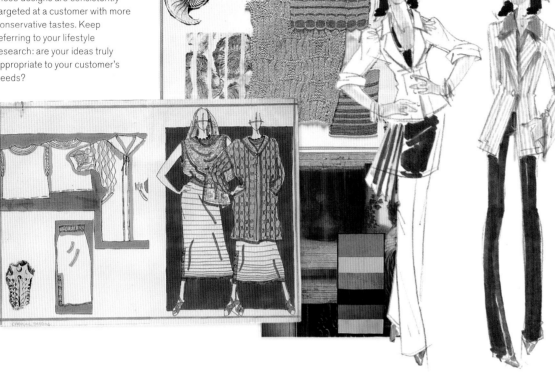

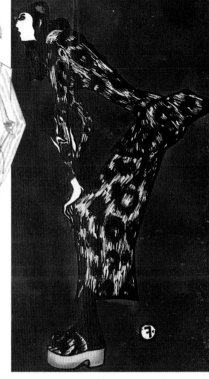

▲ MATCHING DESIGN TO PERSONALITY
An extroverted customer might inspire you to illustrate in a style that displays exaggerated poses and proportions as well as bold silhouettes and fabrics.

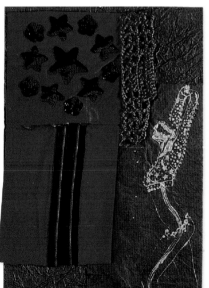

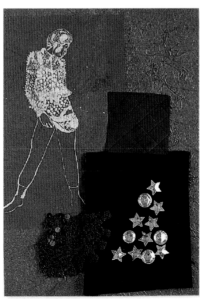

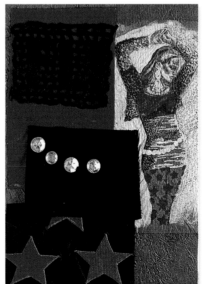

◀ PRESENTATION
Your presentation should reflect the customer profile; here, both design and presentation are targeted at a young, extroverted customer.

UNIT 17 Customer focus

garment. It is the designer's challenge to satisfy the desires of the customer, and there is little room for self-indulgence.

Designers have to strike a delicate balance between appealing to their own tastes and pleasing their customers. Good design and design that appeals to a designer personally are not necessarily the same thing. As the garments illustrated here demonstrate, being a successful fashion designer is not about creating wildly flamboyant costumes that look great on the page but are impossible to wear, but about channeling fashion sense and originality into a customer-targeted outcome.

It is important for a designer to build up a profile of the target customer. This should influence all aspects of the collection, including fabric, color, cost, the formal or casual nature of the garments, and the style of presentation. Clothes are about far more than keeping warm—they are a signal to others of what we feel about ourselves. Understanding the client and the client's aspirations means understanding what messages he or she would like to give out. A successful collection is perfectly constructed to reflect these signals and so to satisfy the customer.

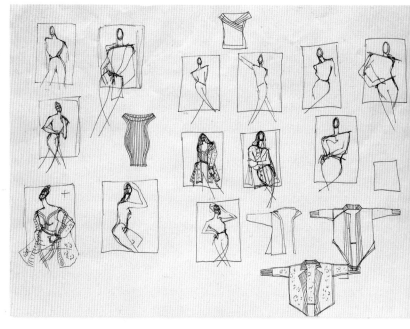

▲ **FOCUSED ROUGHS**
Once the lifestyle of the chosen customer was identified, rough sketches were used to explore initial ideas about when and where different garments might be worn.

▶ **THE PROCESS OF SELECTION**
The strongest of the first ideas were selected to sketch in more detail. These knitwear designs were appropriate to the relaxed daywear needs of the target customer.

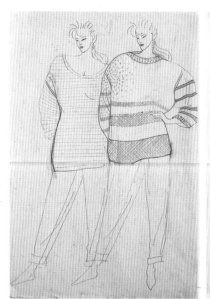

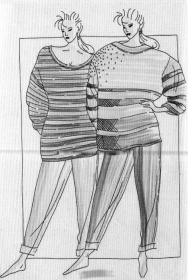

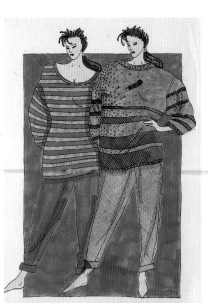

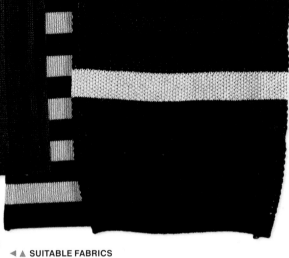

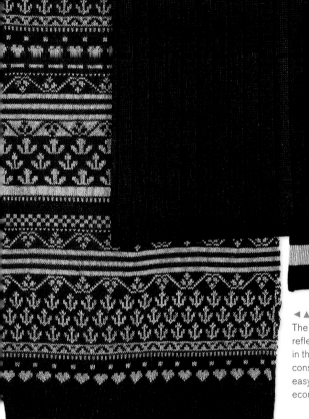

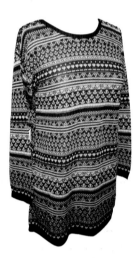

◀ ▲ SUITABLE FABRICS

The lifestyle of the customer should be reflected in the choice of fabrics as well as in the garment silhouette. It is important to consider whether the fabric needs to be easy care, suitable for packing, stretchy, economical, or very comfortable.

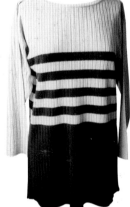

▶ THE RIGHT FIT

The fit of a design is also lifestyle-related. The garment might be figure-hugging or it may have a more comfortable, casual look.

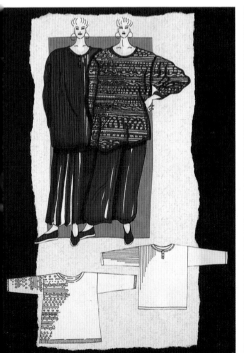

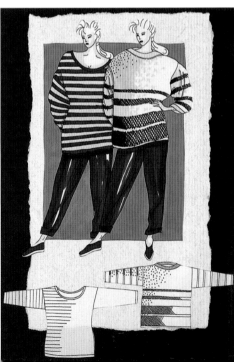

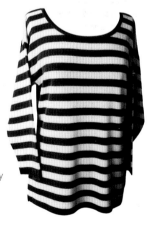

◀ TARGETED PRESENTATION

Commercial designs are often best represented by a clear and simple presentation style.

UNIT 18 Occasions, seasons, budgets

Now that you have begun to understand the lifestyle and aspirations of your customer, the next step is to refine your research still further and make your collection even more focused. A commercial designer will often focus on just one element of a client's lifestyle, perhaps for an eveningwear, lingerie, or swimwear range. It is also important to establish whether your collection will appear in the summer or winter, because this obviously will influence choice of fabric and garment style. The size of your client's budget is another important factor. There is no use creating a wonderful collection of garments if they are

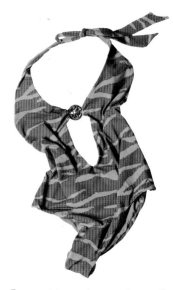

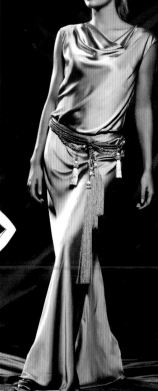

Swimwear made for the pool tends to come in performance fabrics and sportswear colors. Beachwear is more relaxed and often features playful patterns such as florals or animal prints.

▶ **NIGHTLIFE CHOICES**
Female customers may want eveningwear to give an impression of glamour and sophistication, while male formal garments are often more sober. Remember to keep referring to your lifestyle research.

the project
Continue building the customer profile that you began in the last unit, focusing on certain specialized aspects. Also consider the season during which the customer will be wearing your clothes, and the size of the customer's budget. Sketch your rough ideas, stopping from time to time to revisit this initial research. Then finalize a collection of eight targeted garment illustrations.

the objective
● Take your research a step further to explore specialized aspects of the customer's lifestyle.

● Design garments that are appropriate for their end use.
● Consider season and budget.
● Channel your inspirational ideas into a commercially targeted outcome.

the process
Look back at the research you compiled in the last unit about the lifestyle of your target customer. Using words or found images from fashion magazines, continue to build up the story, this time taking the research further to encompass specialized aspects, such as sporting or vacation activities, or special occasions, such as parties or weddings. Should the garments be formal or casual? Are the fabrics you are using appropriate to a specific end use? Sportswear, for instance, must be constructed from a fabric that performs well under extreme conditions and can withstand a great deal of washing.

Also consider the season. Are the fabrics warm enough for winter or can you make use of layering? Your ideas can be put to different seasonal uses; for instance, a shape created in boned satin for a spring collection could be

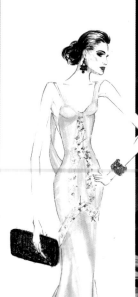

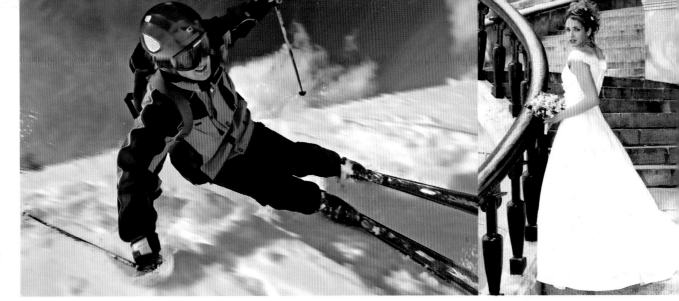

▼ ▶ TECHNICAL INNOVATIONS
Developing active sportswear can be very expensive because these pieces are specialized, incorporating high-performance fabrics.

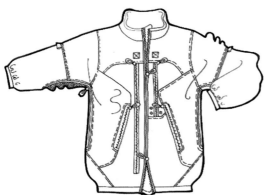

▼ USING SPECIAL FABRICS
Sportswear must stretch and mold around the body and should be easy to wash. The stretchy qualities of sports fabrics also make them ideal for use in fashionable maternity designs.

▲ CUSTOMER ASPIRATIONS
A wedding outfit should always steal the show on the bride's special day.

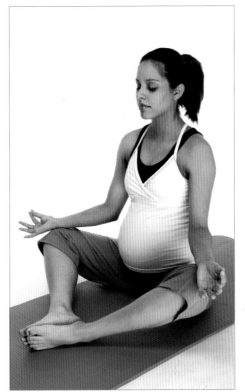

re-created in thick wool for winter, or an embroidery idea on soft chiffon could be translated onto a heavy velvet drape.

How much your clothes will sell for will also dictate how they are made. Is there a great deal of handwork? Are the fabrics expensive? Will the garments have to be dry-cleaned? Would your customer be willing to pay more for all of these things? During production, these kinds of factors are

constantly revisited as pilot garments are produced and, if necessary, styles revised to allow the designs to remain within the appropriate costs.

Once again, check your ideas against the detailed customer research. Can you imagine your customer wearing these garments in the way that you intend? Finally, draw up eight finished outfits.

SELF-CRITIQUE
● Have you truly got inside the mind and lifestyle of your target customer?
● Has the collection evolved toward your research and away from your personal taste?
● Looking back over your research, can you imagine your customer wearing the clothes in a real-life situation?
● Are your final designs truly appropriate for the occasion, season, and budget?

SEE ALSO
● Creating a cohesive collection, p. 92
● Planning a range, p. 98
● Customer focus, p. 104

UNIT 18 Occasions, seasons, budgets

not affordable. Furthermore, a customer with high aspirations will not want clothes that do not give off the right signals about status and wealth.

It would be wrong for a student to start off with a predetermined set of restrictions; the emphasis of this book is on using research to spark ideas. However, once creativity has started to flow, it can be channeled into a commercial outcome. The cost of clothes to the customer is a particularly important factor, although one that is often ignored by students. Designers create garments to be sold: if their prices are exorbitantly high, their collections will not sell. Anyone can create beautiful designs if money is no object, but it requires a talented designer to find the best possible creative solution within a tight budget.

The designs illustrated here show a strong sense of the target customer, and of where and when the client would wear the garments. The collections have credibility because they are well researched: they are stylish and original, yet also consistent with the needs of the customer and the season, and could be sold at an affordable price.

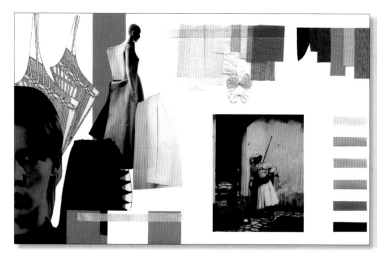

▲ **THOROUGH RESEARCH**
Producing work for a specific occasion and customer might require the compilation of a new, more targeted mood board.

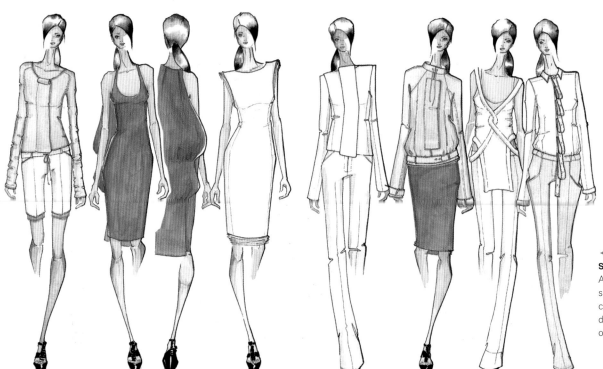

◄ **CONTEMPORARY SPORTSWEAR**
All of these garments are suitable for a sophisticated customer, but can be worn in different ways, as career-wear or urban daywear, for example.

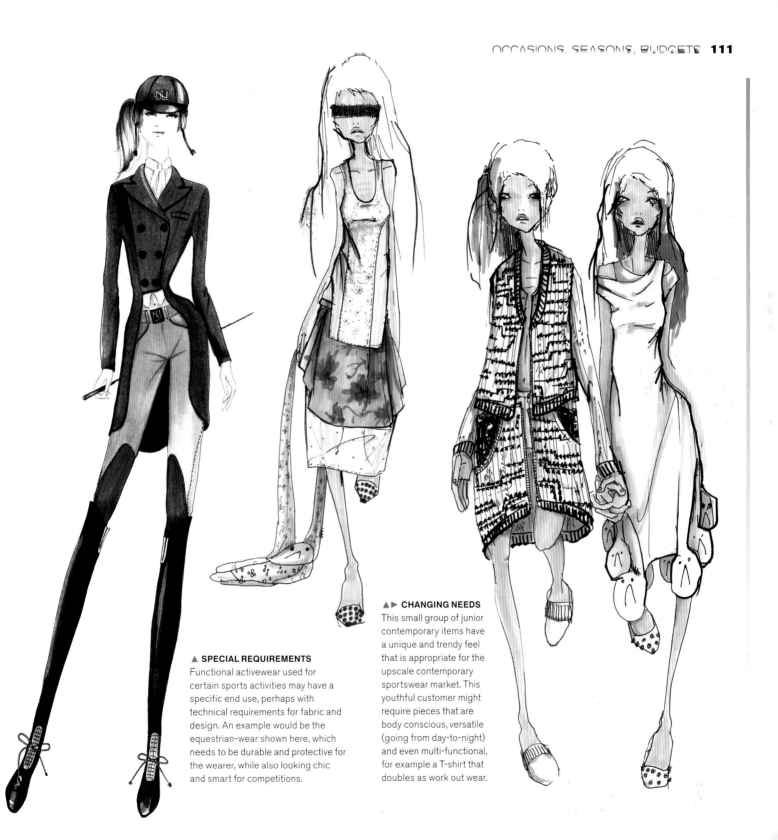

▲ SPECIAL REQUIREMENTS
Functional activewear used for
certain sports activities may have a
specific end use, perhaps with
technical requirements for fabric and
design. An example would be the
equestrian-wear shown here, which
needs to be durable and protective for
the wearer, while also looking chic
and smart for competitions.

▲▶ CHANGING NEEDS
This small group of junior
contemporary items have
a unique and trendy feel
that is appropriate for the
upscale contemporary
sportswear market. This
youthful customer might
require pieces that are
body conscious, versatile
(going from day-to-night)
and even multi-functional,
for example a T-shirt that
doubles as work out wear.

inspiration file

Color and fabric

Two of the most important factors influencing your designs will be your choice of color and fabric. The same shape or garment silhouette remade in another color or fabric will give a totally different effect.

* What season are you designing for? Color palettes and fabric types change depending on the time of year.

* What are the properties of your fabric? A warm and heavy fabric will give a different silhouette to a light and drapey fabric.

Color palettes change from season to season. Not only do individual colors move in and out of favor, with brown becoming "the new black," but there are also subtle evolutions in the shades of colors used. Every designer needs to be aware of the predicted color trends for forthcoming seasons. The fashion industry shares this knowledge through trade shows, style web sites, and magazines—which is how similar ranges of colors appear in our stores each season as if by magic. The cynic might suggest that this is the fashion industry's clever way of encouraging sales, as customers dash out to buy this winter's red dress or pink sweater. However, the evolution is also a natural process. Fashion is charged with reflecting how people feel about themselves and the world around them, and just as themes and inspirations come and go, so too do color palettes. Fabric choice also changes cyclically because certain textiles move in and out of fashion and also because the properties of

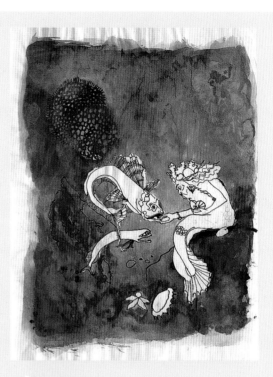

▶ **THINKING IN THREE DIMENSIONS**
You should consider the behavior of fabric on the body right from the start of the creative process, so experiment by draping your chosen fabric on a stand.

▲▶ **MATCHING THE SOURCE**
You could try out color ideas by painting paper first; you may then wish to experiment with dyeing fabric to achieve the exact shade. The colors in this painting were reproduced as samples of dyed fabric, providing the basis for two sets of color selections (right), from which color palettes were later established.

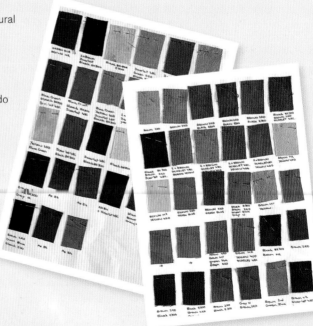

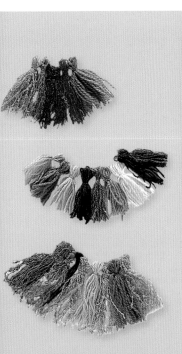

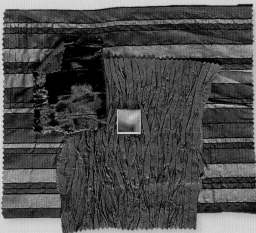

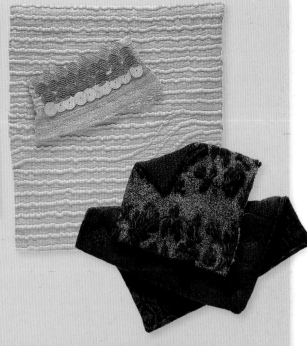

◄▲ HARMONIOUS GROUPINGS
Gather samples of any fabrics, trims, and yarns that you are considering using to establish how different textures as well as colors will work together.

performance or warmth of different fabrics are strongly associated with particular seasons.

Fabric and silhouette cannot be separated. The drape and behavior of your chosen fabric will have a direct effect on the appearance of your garment. Imagine remaking an existing style in a different fabric. What would be the effect of its bulk, stiffness, transparency, softness, fluidity, or tendency to crease? Jeans made in satin or swimwear made of fur would become very different concepts.

You need to consider your choice of fabric carefully at rough-sketch stage. It is not enough to design shapes and then look for a fabric that will give you the right effect. Sensitivity to your materials and the development of shape should take place simultaneously because fabric and silhouette are dependent upon each other.

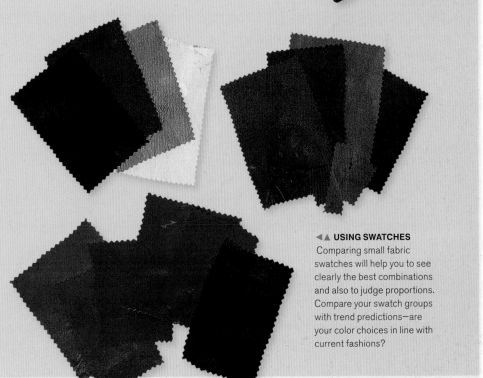

◄▲ USING SWATCHES
Comparing small fabric swatches will help you to see clearly the best combinations and also to judge proportions. Compare your swatch groups with trend predictions—are your color choices in line with current fashions?

UNIT 19 Digital fabric and colorways

As with other areas of design, computer software can be used to create textile design: prints and patterns, weave, texture, and colorways. Colorways are the variety of colors or prints a given fabric comes in. For example, a striped fabric can be produced with different stripe colors. Major manufacturers and companies use proprietary textile design software programs that are costly and task-specific; however, for the purposes of general design, both Adobe Photoshop and Illustrator can be used to create fabrics from scratch, or to modify existing fabrics.

One of the advantages of creating digital fabrics is the ability to choose from exact color systems such as Pantone colors, which are universally recognized and based on mathematical premixes of CMYK values that produce consistent results. These colors can be saved in the "swatches" palettes and applied precisely to fabric swatches, easily creating and reproducing the desired colorway every time. The "Eyedropper" tool in Photoshop, for example, samples a certain color and selects a new foreground or background color to match it. Another benefit of creating digital fabrics is that once the design is created, it can also be applied to a variety of garments. Compare that to free-hand illustration, where you have to re-render the same fabric each time you want to apply it to a new design.

You can create your digital files in different color formats, two of which are RGB and CMYK. RGB is the

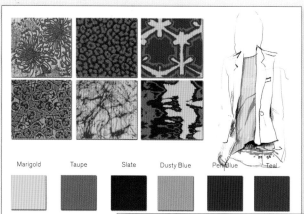

Marigold　Taupe　Slate　Dusty Blue　Peri Blue　Teal

◄ **FOCAL POINT**
This example features colors that are mixed with motifs in a creative way. The illustration adds to the design layout and attracts our attention with the bright yellow shirt as a focal point.

► **LEADING THE EYE**
This example employs a "transition" technique between the color swatches and illustrations. A colorway based on subtle tone and shade variations of complementary colors creates a composition that leads the viewer's eye to where the designer wants it to go.

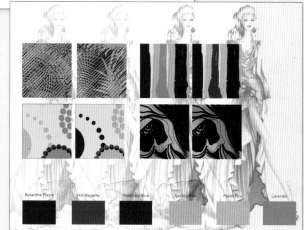

Byzantine Purple　Hot Magenta　Palatinate Blue　Spanish Blue　Pastel Pink　Lavender

the project
Use Adobe Photoshop to create different colorways of the same fabric through a process called "color reduction method," essentially reducing the total number of existing colors in the fabric, and altering color individually.

the objective
● Use digital software to change fabric colors.
● Create a harmonious color palette.
● Understand Adobe Photoshop's color panel, RGB values, and CMYK percentages.
● Utilize the "Eyedropper"

tool in matching exact colors.

the process
1 Research and create a desired color palette containing five shades.
2 Scan a fabric that has a maximum of three different color varieties

in its design. A good example is a leopard print, or a simple floral design.
3 Reduce the number of colors in your fabric. Change the image to "Indexed color" mode. Go to "Image" menu and select Mode>Indexed color. You'll be asked to

flatten layers; select "Ok."
4 Set the parameters. In the "Indexed color panel," choose the following:
Parameters>Palette> Local (adaptive)> Colors> 4 to 6—choose as few as possible without losing color

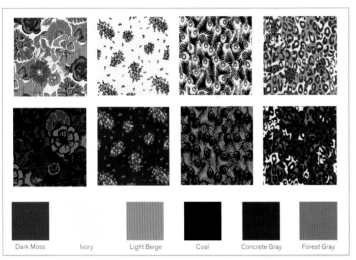

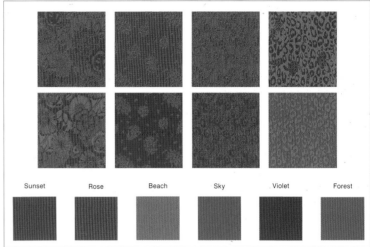

| Dark Moss | Ivory | Light Beige | Coal | Concrete Gray | Forest Gray |

| Sunset | Rose | Beach | Sky | Violet | Forest |

▲ CREATING COLORWAYS

Adobe Photoshop is used here to create different colorways of the four different fabrics in this set. The colorways on the right are based on a more vibrant color palette, whereas the color theme on the left is based on gray scale and neutral tones.

▶ DETECTING COLOR IN PATTERNED FABRIC

Any fabric pattern can be scanned to create colorways. There are four visible colors in this leopard print fabric. Use the "Color picker" panel in Adobe Photoshop to find the desired colors, and the "Eyedropper" tool to select them. Alter as desired.

Choose the color you wish to change using the "Eyedropper" tool. Color percentages appear in the percentage boxes.

The hexadecimal color number can be copied for future reference and color matching.

Change the color as desired (in this case the beige was changed to green) and begin to fill selected areas.

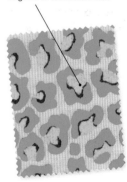

information; Forced> none; Transparency> unchecked; Dither> none. Select "Ok."

5 Change color. Go to Menu and select Mode>Color table. In the "Color table" panel, using the "Color picker," change the color swatches to the colors of your choice. Play with the color choices until you achieve the desired hue and shade. Use the color palette you created in the first step as a selection guide.

6 While in the "Color picker" panel, observe the values for RGB and CMYK and the hexadecimal color number.

7 Revert the image. You need to revert to the original image mode to regain resolution. To change the image mode back to RGB, select Image > Mode > RGB.

8 Repeat the process to create a total of five different colorways based on your original palette. Use the "Eyedropper" tool to match the colors of your palette.

SELF-CRITIQUE
- Did you match the colors accurately?
- Did you try different color combinations (in your colorway) for the prints?

UNIT 19 Digital fabric and colorways

▼ CREATE SEAMLESS DIGITAL PATTERNS

When a motif or design is "Designed as pattern" in Adobe Photoshop or Illustrator, these programs tile the motif, repeating it to fill the selected object or garment. A "seamless pattern" is one where, when applied to a garment, the rendering will be continuous and uniform, and where no seams or edges are visible between the tiled patterns.

Red, Green, and Blue light file setting used when viewing files on a computer monitor or the web. CMYK is the Cyan, Magenta, Yellow, and Black pigments setting used for files that are to be printed. Although many printers convert RGB to CMYK settings for printing, for the most accurate color results, it's a good idea to convert your RGB to CMYK in Photoshop before printing your file (so that you can see how the image will print and adjust colors as needed). To do so, go to Menu>Image>Mode>RGB or CMYK.

When fabric swatches are scanned or photographed with a digital camera, they have many more colors than are needed. With a software program like Photoshop, it is possible to reduce and manipulate the number of colors.

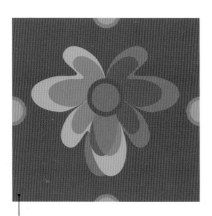

Create your design using Adobe Illustrator's "Pen" and "Pencil" tools with different "Fill" and "Stroke" colors and opacities.

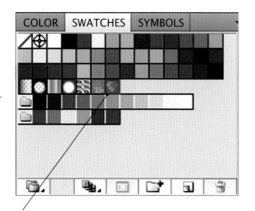

Drag the motif into the "Swatches" panel to make it a new pattern. Now any closed path can be rendered with this floral print.

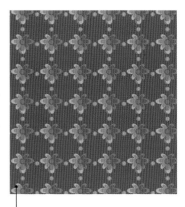

Create a rectangle, and while the rectangle is selected, click on the newly-created "swatch" and the shape will be filled with the chosen swatch.

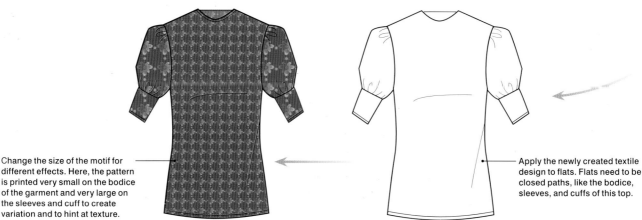

Change the size of the motif for different effects. Here, the pattern is printed very small on the bodice of the garment and very large on the sleeves and cuff to create variation and to hint at texture.

Apply the newly created textile design to flats. Flats need to be closed paths, like the bodice, sleeves, and cuffs of this top.

▶ **EXPERIMENT**
Garments can be rendered using a variety of vector patterns. Use the same garment shape, such as this simple vest top, as a template to experiment with various pattern designs of all colors.

▼ **DEFAULT SWATCH PALETTES**
Knowing how to create your own patterns affords you unique and innovative textile design. However, a variety of patterns can be found in Adobe Illustrator's default "Swatch" palettes and many, created by other designers, can be downloaded from the Internet.

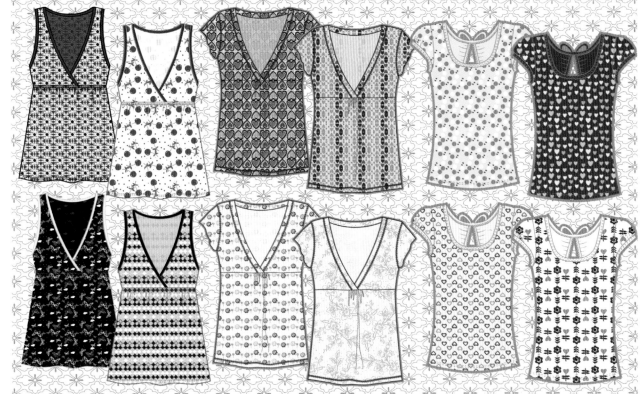

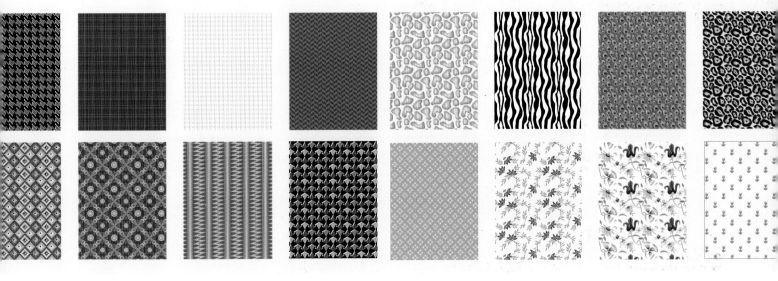

UNIT 20 Color palettes

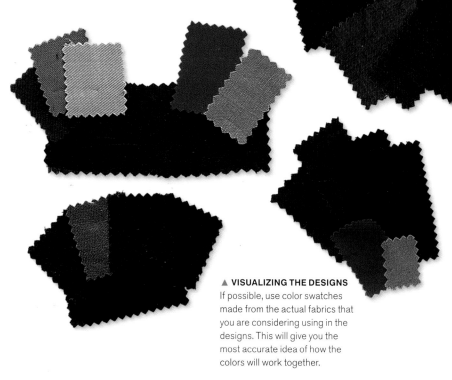

A palette is a limited selection of colors that a designer uses in a collection to ensure that all the color elements sit together in a controlled way. Restricting yourself to a set of colors is an important part of the creative process: a garment or outfit can be totally reinvented by merely changing its colors.

The more colors you include in a palette the more challenging it is to use. A limited palette ensures that designs have a natural continuity. As a rule of thumb, novice designers should avoid palettes with more than eight colors. As you gain experience, the number of colors you use will become a matter of personal choice in keeping with your design style.

When creating a color palette, many students and designers use the reference books of tear-out color chips produced by Pantone. These uniformly sized color blocks are convenient to use and look tidy on a mood or presentation board. All the colors have individual reference numbers, recognized throughout the fashion industry, which you can quote when talking to clients, dyers, or manufacturers to avoid confusion about exactly which shades you mean.

Establishing a color palette first and then using it in

▲ **VISUALIZING THE DESIGNS**
If possible, use color swatches made from the actual fabrics that you are considering using in the designs. This will give you the most accurate idea of how the colors will work together.

◄▼ **EXPERIMENT FIRST**
Working from your rough ideas, create simple outline sketches of your collection. These can then be photocopied a number of times so that you can try out various color combinations.

the project
Isolate the important colors from your research and create color chips (or use the Pantone shades) to select a palette. Then use the palette as a focus while you are designing a collection. As you sketch out designs, vary the combination and proportion of colors used within the garments and outfits. Assess the balance of colors within the collection as a whole.

Then create eight final drawings, using the most successful color combinations.

the objective
● Establish a working color palette.
● Vary the combination of colors to see how this affects the designs.
● Develop a collection with a successful color balance.

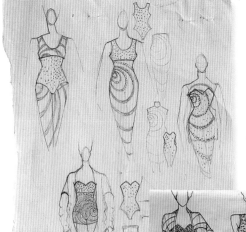

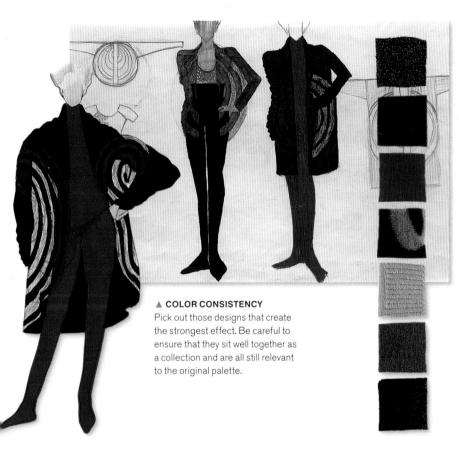

▲ **COLOR CONSISTENCY**
Pick out those designs that create the strongest effect. Be careful to ensure that they sit well together as a collection and are all still relevant to the original palette.

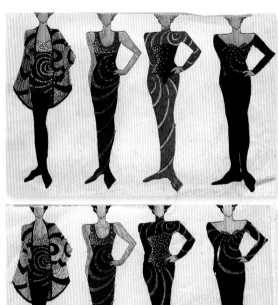

▲ **PLAYING WITH PROPORTION**
Varying the proportion and combination of colors can give a strikingly different look to the same design. Try out a number of variations.

the process

Your mood board will suggest the important colors for your theme. Isolate these as color chips—either use Pantone chips or make your own from small squares of fabric, magazine cuttings, paint, or samples of yarn wrapped around a card. Use anything that shows a flat area of color, but avoid patterns. Start to group the chips into a palette, remembering that it is easier to use no more than eight colors.

It is very important to adhere to your palette as you sketch out your design ideas. Start by drawing roughs in black-and-white outline form; photocopy these and color each set differently, using your palette.

Dramatic color combinations produce exciting results, so be daring! Try using colors in different proportions.

Combinations that work well in a palette can be ruined by an ill-considered use of proportion. For example, a black velvet evening dress with a side split can look fantastic with an occasionally glimpsed red lining. However, the same dress in red and black stripes would not be at all as sophisticated.

Always keep your research in mind and try to evoke a similar use of color in your designs. Finally, draw eight outfits, using the most successful color combinations from your rough experiments.

SELF-CRITIQUE
● Have you established a focused and workable color palette?
● Do you see a link between the colors in your research and those in your final designs?

SEE ALSO
● Mood boards, p. 28
● Designing fabric ideas, p. 48

UNIT 21 Color palettes

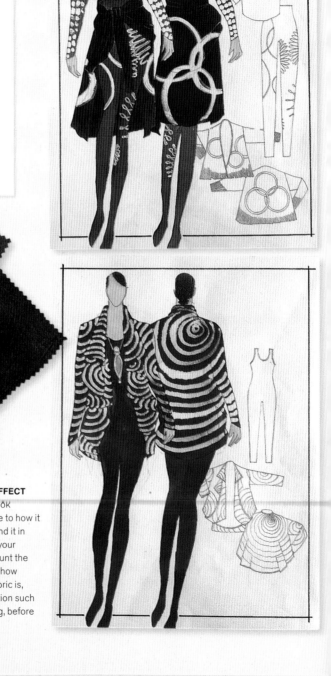

the generation of roughs and final drawings ensures a consistent set of designs, as demonstrated here. Adjusting the proportion of colors can put a new spin on an illustration, giving it an individual feel while still tying it into the collection as a whole through the use of a common palette. Even more dramatic effects can be achieved by applying an entirely new color palette.

These illustrations could be recolored by scanning them into a computer and substituting new colors, by feeding the outlines through a color photocopier and adjusting the color balance, or by redrawing or photocopying the designs and repainting them. Changing the color palette will alter the whole look of a range: the same floral design might be colored in greens for a high summer jungle story, in pinks for a spring feminine theme, or in blue and white for a nautical feel.

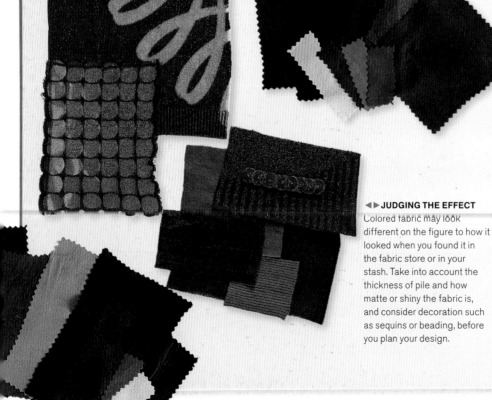

◀▶ JUDGING THE EFFECT
Colored fabric may look different on the figure to how it looked when you found it in the fabric store or in your stash. Take into account the thickness of pile and how matte or shiny the fabric is, and consider decoration such as sequins or beading, before you plan your design.

◄ ► ▼ VARIATIONS ON A THEME
These final illustrations reflect the original palette, although the proportions of colors used have been varied from garment to garment to give each one an individual identity.

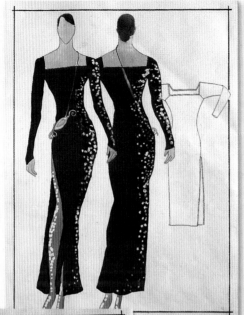

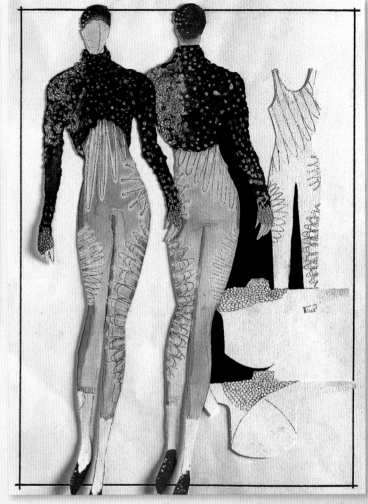

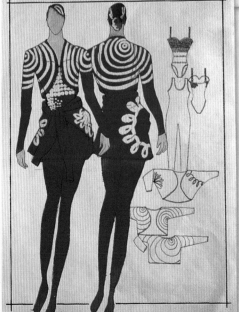

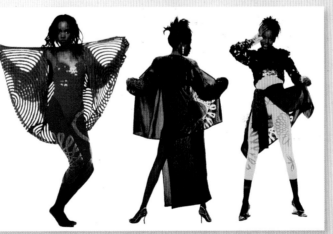

◄ BREAKING THE RULES
Cohesion is a positive foundation for a palette, but adding a surprising splash of a primary color like yellow in an unexpected or bold shade can lend a sense of drama to a design.

UNIT 21 Structuring fabric

We have seen how important choice of color is to the outcome of a project. Fabric has a similar impact and needs to be as carefully considered. Unit 8 (pages 52–55) discussed how a fabric embellishment idea can be the focus for a design; this unit will look at how the structuring of fabric can drive garment construction, whether through methods such as pleating, draping, or binding, or through the creation of entirely new fabric structures using techniques such as crochet, knitting, or appliqué. As you gain experience, you will see how fabrics have particular properties and behave in very different ways. You need to learn to harness the inherent properties of fabrics, whether you are working with clinging jersey, chunky knits, or high-performance sportswear. As your confidence grows, you will want to control the effect of fabric from the earliest stages of the design process. Then, rather than relying on store-purchased textiles to fit your theme, you will be able to manipulate fabric to dictate the volume and shape of your garments, as well as their surface appearance and texture.

The construction of these garments has been driven by the structuring of fabric, whether through the building up of new textiles or the manipulation of existing fabric to create volume and shape. Designers

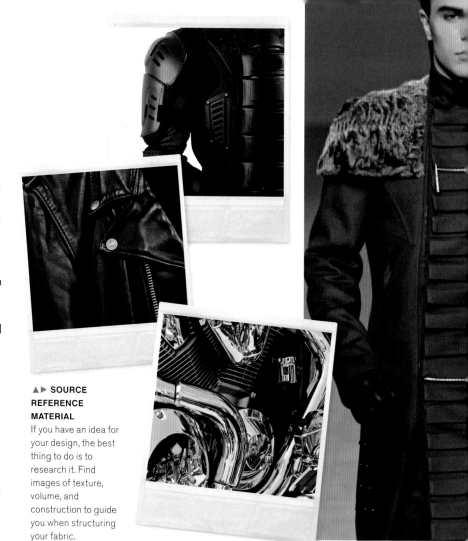

▲▶ **SOURCE REFERENCE MATERIAL**
If you have an idea for your design, the best thing to do is to research it. Find images of texture, volume, and construction to guide you when structuring your fabric.

the project

As you put together a mood board and color palette, experiment with structuring fabric to create a silhouette. Explore your ideas by manipulating paper; then consider how these ideas can be transferred onto fabric, either through techniques, such as pleating and draping, or through methods that create an entirely new fabric structure. Choose the strongest roughs to create a final collection that incorporates your fabric structuring ideas.

the objective

● Take an active role in fabric manipulation.
● Develop structuring ideas that drive your designs.
● Ensure your fabric development is in line with fashion trends.

the process

Gather research images using drawing and photography, and identify the key shapes and structures. Treating your page as a piece of fabric, start to sketch out structuring ideas. Don't worry at this stage about the practicalities of achieving the effects; just let your imagination run wild. Still working on paper, experiment with methods such as gluing, stapling, hand and machine stitching, cutouts, and appliqué. Remember that you are looking for ideas that will support the construction of the garments.

Now think about how these first thoughts can be translated onto fabric. You could create a fastening using fabric ties. Stitching and gluing could be the means of structuring a finished garment or might provide seaming ideas. Layering, pleating, and draping are all ways of creating volume in a garment. You might consider how cutting fabric on the bias (placing pattern pieces at a

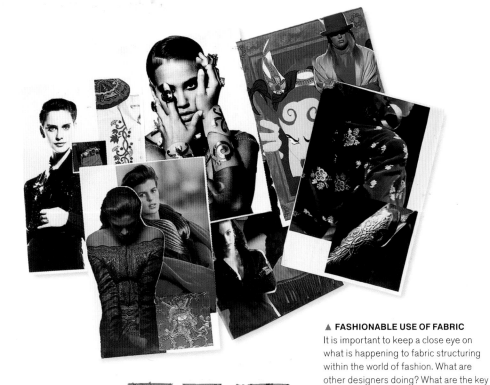

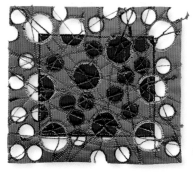

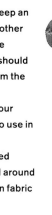

▲ FASHIONABLE USE OF FABRIC
It is important to keep a close eye on what is happening to fabric structuring within the world of fashion. What are other designers doing? What are the key trends? Such considerations will stop you from becoming overly self-indulgent.

▲◄ BUILDING A NEW FABRIC
You can structure fabric by attaching small pieces together to create an overall design. Explore these ideas on paper.

45-degree angle to the fabric selvages and grain) would affect structure. Bias-cut fabric has far greater drape than usual, and clings to the body in a very flattering and feminine way when used in skirts and dresses.

You could even build up a completely new fabric, using techniques such as crochet, patchwork, or knitting.

Remember to keep an eye on the work of other designers. All these wonderful effects should not distract you from the fashion overview.

Finally, select your strongest roughs to use in putting together a collection of finished designs structured around your experiments in fabric manipulation and distortion.

SELF-CRITIQUE
● Have you created unique and original structuring ideas?
● Does your fabric manipulation reflect your research?
● Are the fabrics appropriate for your intended audience?

SEE ALSO
● Designing fabric ideas, p. 48
● Color palettes, p. 118

UNIT 21 Structuring fabric

need to be aware of the structural nature of different fabrics and incorporate them into their fashion ideas accordingly. Bulky knitwear, for example, can be designed only into certain shapes, and is bound to be heavy and hot. Clinging jerseys, on the other hand, will mold around the body, and fine velvets will drape into soft folds. The behavior of fabric can be explored by molding samples around the curves of a dressmaker's stand, or around a real body. If the fabric has a complex structure—an ornate crocheted pattern, for example—it is important to remember that the silhouette should be kept simple in order to avoid a confused overall effect.

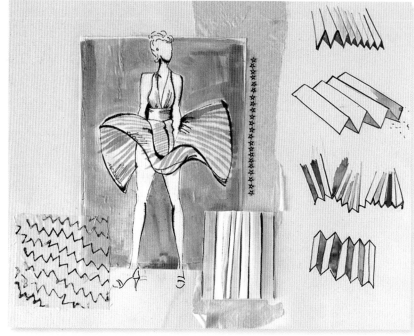

▲ VOLUME ON THE BODY
Methods of fabric manipulation such as folding, pleating, and draping can be used to give volume and shape to relatively simple fabrics. Make sketches from your findings to better your understanding of how different fabrics work.

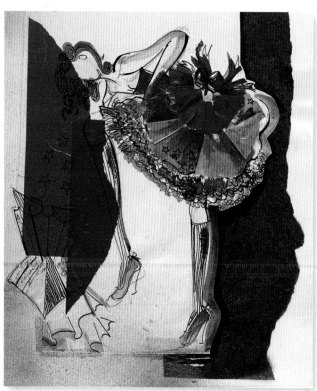

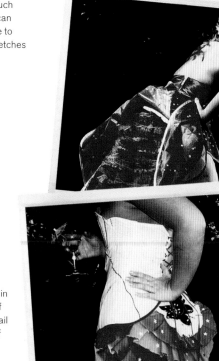

◀▶ LAYERING FOR EFFECT
The layering of a different fabric in a contrasting color at the back of this bodice adds volume and detail to the relatively plain structure of the overall dress.

Embellishments

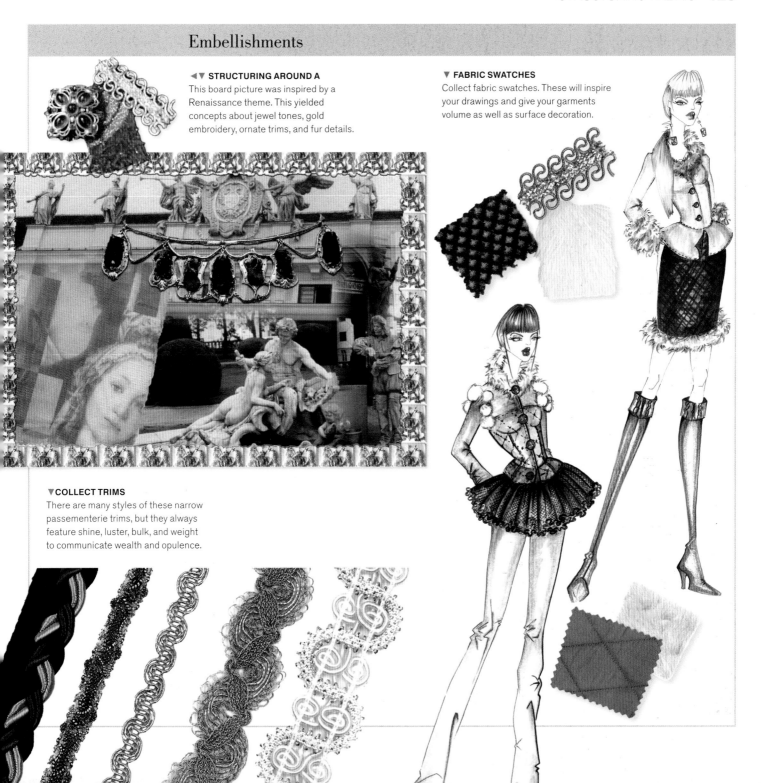

◀▼ STRUCTURING AROUND A

This board picture was inspired by a Renaissance theme. This yielded concepts about jewel tones, gold embroidery, ornate trims, and fur details.

▼ FABRIC SWATCHES

Collect fabric swatches. These will inspire your drawings and give your garments volume as well as surface decoration.

▼ COLLECT TRIMS

There are many styles of these narrow passementerie trims, but they always feature shine, luster, bulk, and weight to communicate wealth and opulence.

4 Communicating your vision

The most wonderful ideas and stylish drawing techniques will count for nothing if you cannot present your designs effectively. This chapter explains how to support your illustrations with flat working drawings and represent your ideas as three-dimensional garments. You will also learn how to create professional-looking presentation boards, to choose the most appropriate illustration style for your work, and to communicate your vision clearly, accurately, and with maximum impact.

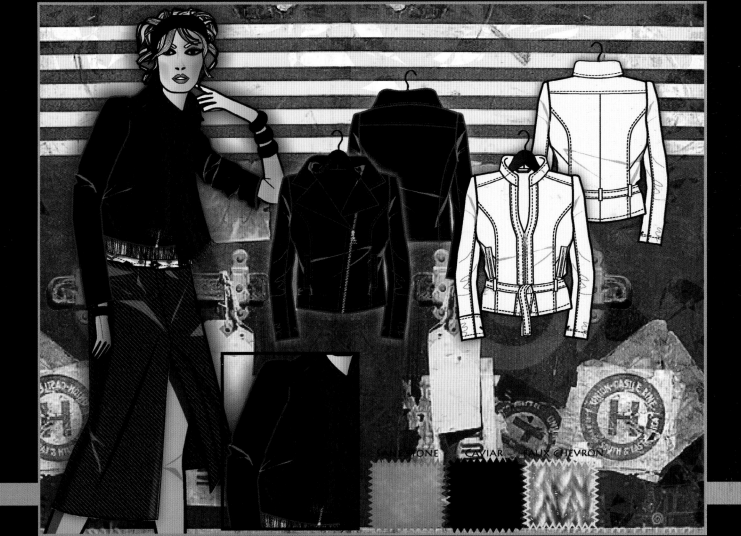

SANDSTONE   CAVIAR   FAUX CHEVRON

inspiration file

Clarity and communication

* Just how critical is clarity to the communication of my design?

* What are "flat drawings" and how do they contribute to my design proposal?

* Can a design be produced from sample through production pattern to actual garment?

Clarity does not mean that you have to omit creativity. Depending on your style of drawing, your work might be unambiguous or somewhat open to interpretation. Look critically at your finished drawings and decide whether or not they are clear to a first-time observer. If the construction or silhouette is in doubt, technical flat drawings could be provided.

As a commercial designer, working as part of a team, clear communication will be paramount, and you will often find yourself dealing mainly or even wholly with working flat drawings. Fortunately, they are very quick to complete, and with a little practice you can become proficient at these types of drawings.

Flat drawings are referred to in many different ways, such as specification drawings or "specs," technical flat drawings or "tech flats," or any combination of these terms. As the names suggest, these drawings are accurate, clear, and easy-to-understand flat representations of your design ideas. These "flats" are created for production purposes. Like building plans, they are a faithful representation or blueprint of every important construction aspect of a garment. Today, technical flats are created by hand, then digitized, so actual scale is not necessary. Measurements are not always required as long as accurate construction information is provided with the drawings. Necessary design information should be included where appropriate, and illustrations on the figure will support the design concepts along with the flat.

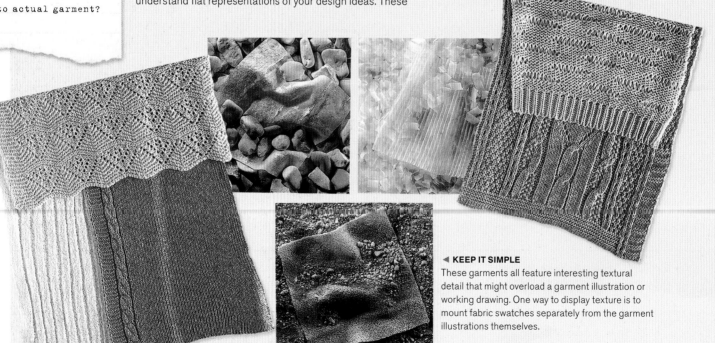

◄ KEEP IT SIMPLE
These garments all feature interesting textural detail that might overload a garment illustration or working drawing. One way to display texture is to mount fabric swatches separately from the garment illustrations themselves.

▶ **CONVEYING TEXTURE**
When depicting very textured
fabrics, such as those pictured
here, you need to maintain a
balance between depicting that
texture and keeping your
illustrations clear. Inspirational
material can be included on a
presentation board to reinforce
the mood of the collection, but
avoid overloading the board with
so much detail that it becomes
confused.

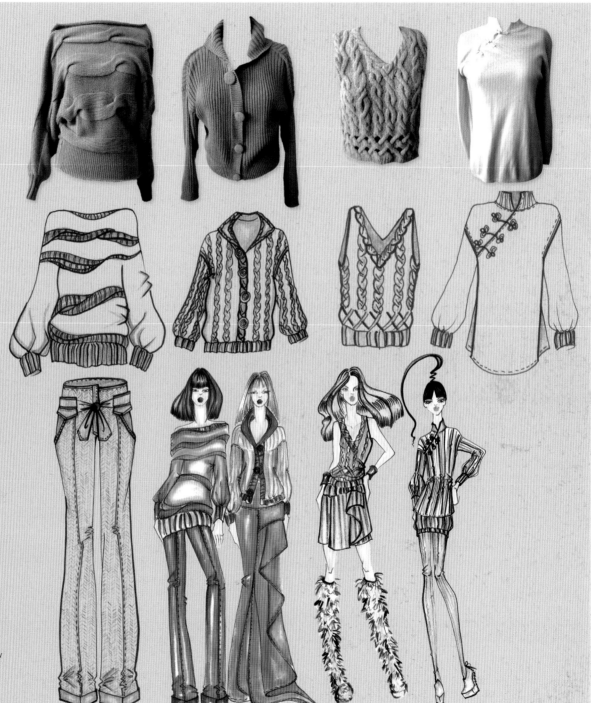

▶ **PROVIDING THE DETAIL**
Flat technical drawings help to
clarify how the illustrated
garments are constructed.
They can also define exactly how
and where surface pattern or
stitch texture is to be placed on
a garment.

UNIT 22 Working drawings

Creative final illustrations of your collection will often need to be supported with clear and accurate flat working drawings. This will allow you to be artistic in your illustrations, knowing that they are supported by technical drawings that provide an unambiguous and precise description of your garments. Your working drawings should record exactly how your clothes are to be constructed, and how all the details, trims, and finishes are to be applied. Completing them will force you to make decisions about these factors, which might otherwise have been left open to interpretation. You

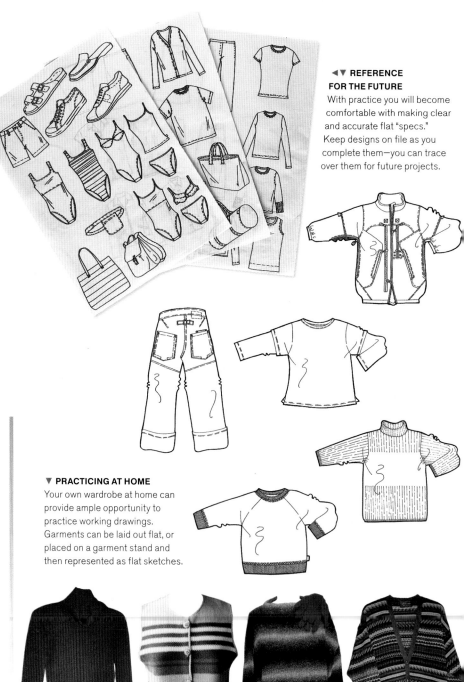

◄▼ REFERENCE FOR THE FUTURE
With practice you will become comfortable with making clear and accurate flat "specs." Keep designs on file as you complete them—you can trace over them for future projects.

▼ PRACTICING AT HOME
Your own wardrobe at home can provide ample opportunity to practice working drawings. Garments can be laid out flat, or placed on a garment stand and then represented as flat sketches.

the project

Look through your wardrobe at home and pull out a range of different types of garment. Lay them out neatly on the floor so that you can observe every detail. Photograph the garments so that you start to relate to them as flat illustrations. Try representing what you see as accurate flat line drawings that clearly describe the construction of the garments and their details. Then practice by making working drawings of your previous illustrations.

the objective

- Assess critically the construction of existing garments.
- Practice making drawings that accurately describe the proportion, makeup, and details of your garments.
- Apply what you have learned to the exact description of previous design illustrations.
- As a result of this process, think in more detail about your designs.

SEE ALSO
● Practicalities of
  presentation, p. 140
● Presenting with
  flair, p. 150

the process

Select a range of your own garments. You could even buy a few items from a thrift store and take them apart to investigate their construction. Work with five garments, choosing a variety of difficult pieces.

You need to be able to look directly down on the clothes from above, rather than at an angle, so lay them out on the floor instead of on a table. Lay them out as simply as possible, with no creases. Avoid overlapping sleeves with garment fronts; either place sleeves to the sides or fold them over on themselves. Take photos of the laid-out garments. These will be easier to draw from and will help you relate to the clothes as flat shapes.

Using a fine black felt-tip pen and working on a layout pad, start to draw exactly what you see. The first few drawings will take the most time to complete. After that you can place one of the initial drawings underneath each fresh page in your pad to use as a starting point as you sketch the next one. This will save you time as you draw the collection, ensuring proportions are kept the same and emphasizing similarities of outline that will give the selection of garments cohesion as an illustrated collection. Remember to describe every aspect of the garments, including their proportions, seam details, trims, pocket positions, necklines and sleeve and body shapes, as well as front and back views. You can outline your drawings with a slightly thicker black pen to highlight the garment silhouette.

If you are finding it difficult to get going, start by tracing in pencil over your photographs and then work over the pencil outlines in pen. In this way, you will build up a set of drawings that you can use as a foundation for other drawings.

Finally, refer to your previous creative illustrations and make working drawings of these. As you take the working drawings back into the creative process, using them as a basis for further developments, you will deepen your understanding of your own designs.

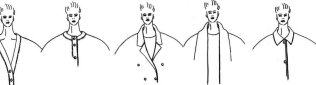

◀ WHEN FIGURES ARE NEEDED
Sometimes details such as necklines need to be represented on the body so that the exact scale and proportion can be shown.

► NOT ALWAYS NECESSARY
Some fashion illustrations might not need to be supplemented with additional flat drawings. If they are clear and unambiguous, they can communicate your design ideas sufficiently on their own.

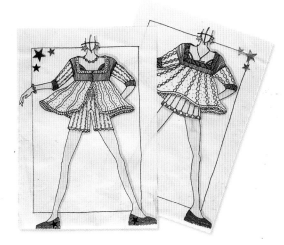

SELF-CRITIQUE
● Have you chosen a challenging range of garments to draw?
● Have you described every aspect of their construction and detailing successfully?
● Show your drawings to someone else and ask them to describe what they see. Does this description match the real garments?
● Do your working drawings describe your designs more accurately than your creative illustrations?

UNIT 22 Working drawings

will be surprised at how the process of making working drawings forces you to think more deeply about your designs.

As the illustrations here demonstrate, they are very useful either mounted on a presentation board, giving details that might otherwise have cluttered up the illustration, or as part of the creative process, representing existing garments to provide a basis for related but original designs. The ability to make working drawings is a useful skill for a designer to show in a portfolio, because commercial designers are more likely to work with this type of drawing than any other. Working drawings should communicate effectively the precise construction, proportion, and embellishment of the design, so much so that they could be handed over to a pattern cutter or machinist in the confidence that the ideas will be re-created exactly.

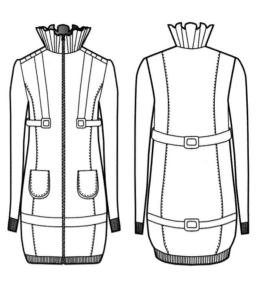

▲▶ SUPPORTING CREATIVITY
These working drawings provide the details, enabling a more creative depiction of the skinny jean and bomber jacket.

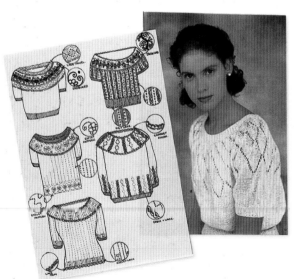

▲▶ REINTERPRETING EXISTING DESIGNS
Using flat working drawings to represent garments featured in fashion magazines may inspire the creation of a range of related but original pieces.

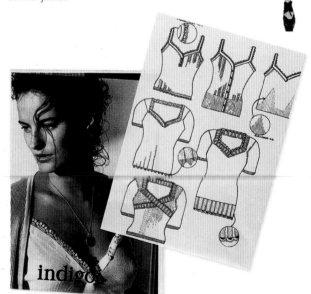

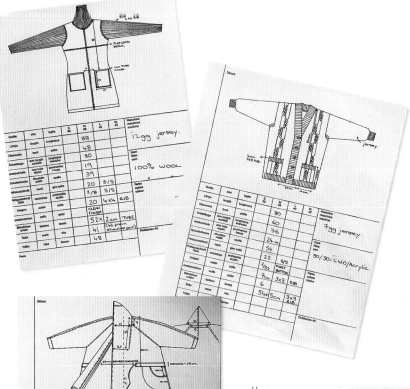

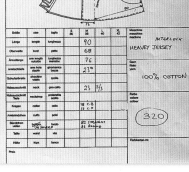

▲ COMMERCIAL DRAWINGS
Specification drawings used for factory production purposes are highly technical and detailed.

▼ SCALE AND PROPORTION
Designers do not always provide measurements for working drawings. It is usually more important to ensure that the representations are to scale and in proportion.

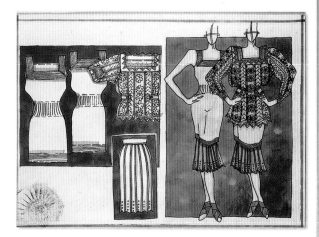

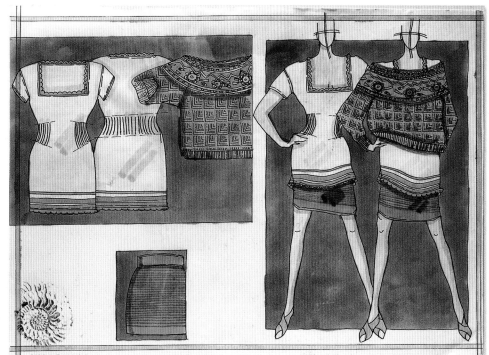

UNIT 23 Real garments for your portfolio

This project will allow you to present your designs as three-dimensional garments. We are not dealing here with the technical aspects of garment construction—that is an involved topic that would fill another book. However, you can still represent a design as a finished piece by mocking up a garment that can then be captured with photography. If you have actually made up any of your designs already, then you will be able to practice styling the garments so that they can be photographed to best effect.

You will find this project to be a wonderful learning experience that will add to your creativity. The best way to learn about garment construction is to practice taking apart and making up real items. You will then become familiar with the shapes of pattern pieces, and methods of seaming and finishing. Draping fabric on a

the project

Select some design illustrations that you would like to represent in garment form. Wrap fabric around a dressmaker's stand or model to create an impression of finished garments that you can capture with photography. If you have already made up garments from some of your illustrations, experiment with different ways of styling clothes and photographing them.

the objective

- Represent real garments in your portfolio.
- Practice styling your designs on a model or a stand.

- Develop design ideas by draping fabrics or garments on a model or a garment stand.

the process

Start with a length of fabric draped over the stand or body and manipulate it as the design dictates, by folding, tying, stretching, binding, or gathering. Aim to mimic the way the fabric would behave on the body if it were constructed as a garment. Pieces can be cut away or pinned in place as the shape of the garment is evolved, but this might not be necessary. Alternatively, experiment with styling and photographing garments

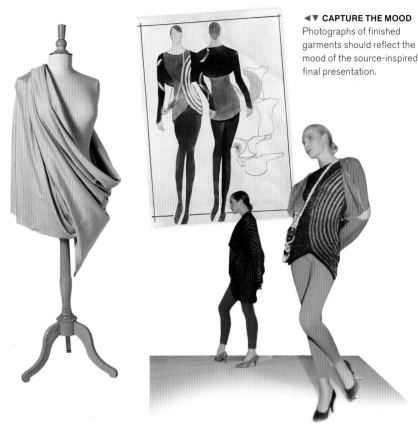

◀▼ CAPTURE THE MOOD
Photographs of finished garments should reflect the mood of the source-inspired final presentation.

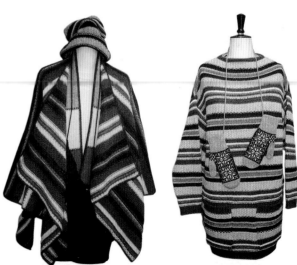

▲▶ STYLING GARMENTS
Experiment with different ways of draping fabrics and accessorizing clothes on the stand. Consider using items such as jewelry, or hats and gloves.

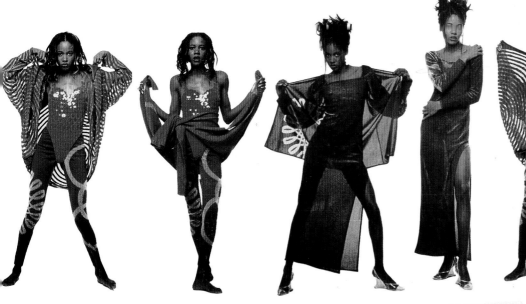

◀ **TEAMWORK**
Why not team up with other students? These photographs were the result of a collaboration between a fashion student, a photography student, and a young model. The images were used in all three portfolios!

▶ **ON THE RUNWAY**
If your college has an end-of-year show, be sure to capture your designs on film and then mount these images for your portfolio.

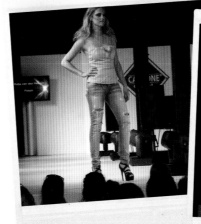

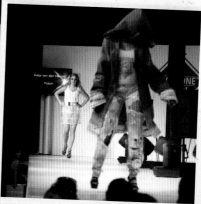

that you have already made up.

While you are working, keep your mind open to new ideas, because the process of folding and draping will encourage you to develop new design solutions. For example, as you are creating pleats of fabric as suggested by an illustration, you might notice that the folds create a scalloped edge on a sleeve, or a drape of fabric over the hips, in a way that you had not anticipated. These sorts of ideas can be incorporated into the range and used on other garments, or reconsidered and exaggerated within the

existing designs. They might even become more important than the original concept. Alternatively, they can be noted down for use in a future project.

Style garments with flair to represent the spirit of the design illustrations. Try out as many options as possible to display your work. You could arrange garments on a model, a stand, a hanger, or laid flat on the floor—clothes have even been photographed on a dog! Experiment with different options and be as creative as you can. Keep in mind what you are trying to achieve: the positive representation of your design concepts.

SEE ALSO
● Customer focus, p. 104
● Presenting with flair, p. 150

SELF-CRITIQUE
● Were you either too ambitious or too safe in your choice of drawings to mock up or finished garments to style?
● Have you used a wide range of methods to mock up and style the garments?
● Do your photographs successfully capture the proportions and styling of the garments?
● Have you avoided amateurish presentation?

UNIT 23 Real garments for your portfolio

dressmaker's stand is another route to garment design, involving observation of how the fabric actually behaves on the body (which can only be imagined at the sketching stage). Some designers work best in this way and start by draping fabric before they even pick up pen and paper.

Photographs of three-dimensional garments, either real or mocked up, take fashion illustration a step further and allow the representation of finished pieces in a portfolio. As shown by some of the images here, the photography does not have to be particularly "arty" to show off the designs to great effect. Using video or still photography to capture designs as they come down the runway at an end-of-year event will give their presentation the feel of a top fashion show. Pieces displayed on a stand or draped around a body can sometimes be best photographed through close-ups of garment sections rather than through a styled photo-shoot approach that could look amateurish if the quality of the photography is not very good (another option is to collaborate with a photographer). The use of a digital camera can be productive, allowing the images to be further manipulated with a computer. The digital editing process can result in new design ideas as well as in creative presentation.

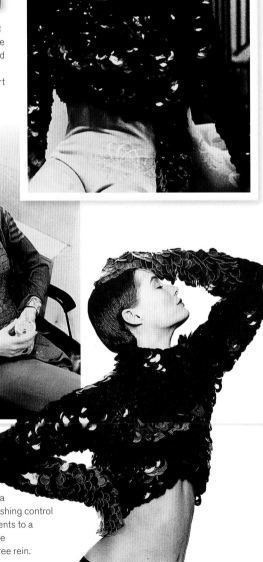

▲ **MONOCHROME OR COLOR**
Working with a black-and-white image rather than color can add sophistication to the piece. Or use this as a tonal guide to start a monochrome drawing.

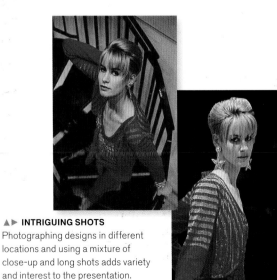

▲▶ **INTRIGUING SHOTS**
Photographing designs in different locations and using a mixture of close-up and long shots adds variety and interest to the presentation.

▲▶ **LETTING GO**
Successful collaboration with a photographer involves relinquishing control over the portrayal of the garments to a certain extent, and allowing the photographer some creative free rein.

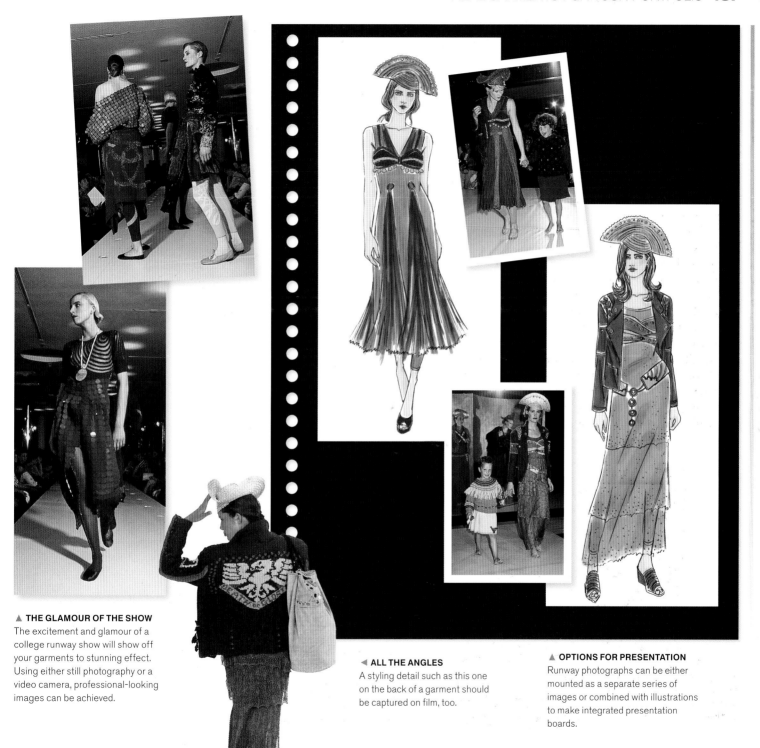

▲ **THE GLAMOUR OF THE SHOW**
The excitement and glamour of a college runway show will show off your garments to stunning effect. Using either still photography or a video camera, professional-looking images can be achieved.

◀ **ALL THE ANGLES**
A styling detail such as this one on the back of a garment should be captured on film, too.

▲ **OPTIONS FOR PRESENTATION**
Runway photographs can be either mounted as a separate series of images or combined with illustrations to make integrated presentation boards.

Presenting your work

Fashion designers are in the business of visual communication, and effective presentation of work is all important. Your brain may be teeming with innovative ideas and you may produce the most original designs, but none of this will matter if you are unable to communicate your vision. In the fashion business, first impressions really do count. When you show your work, you need to ensure that your presentation looks as professional as possible—organized, well mounted, and clean, as well as accurate, clear, and creatively appropriate.

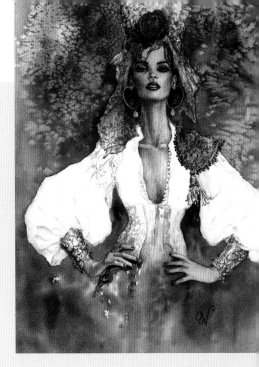

Your illustrations can be mounted on boards or inserted into portfolio sleeves, both of which can be bought from art supply stores. Boards are available in various sizes, and your choice will be influenced by factors such as personal preference or your audience size—larger boards may be appropriate for large group presentations. You could also consider scanning illustrations into a computer and presenting your work in the format of a PowerPoint or digital presentation.

Start out by using A3 (16¼ x 11¾ in./41 x 30 cm) boards and be prepared to try different options. Avoid using a combination of sizes in the actual portfolio, because continuity is important. Work presented must be clean, and make sure that your presentation is current and relevant to the client.

A sturdy portfolio is also essential; this will help to keep your artwork clean and professional looking. Consider getting a few different-sized cases for storage purposes. Plastic sleeves are great for storage and transport; however, they sometimes have a slight sheen or glare, so you may want to consider taking the work out at the time of your presentation.

Consider carefully the style of illustration you choose for the design being presented, as well as your approach to the overall presentation format. These considerations will ultimately allow you to present designs in the most positive and successful way. For example, children's-wear could have a cartoon style and whimsical flair, perhaps even including playful props or pets. All the elements of your presentation should be unified, and continuity is the key. You could even present your sketchbook, since this offers a glimpse into your creative ideas and potential, providing possible employers with insight into your working process.

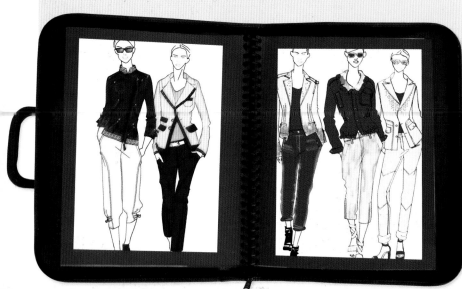

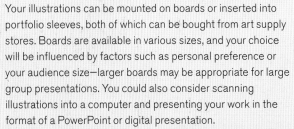

◀ TRANSPORTING PROJECTS
A sturdy portfolio is the safest and most efficient means of transporting work. Build up a collection of different sizes to house all your illustrations.

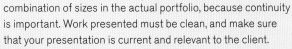

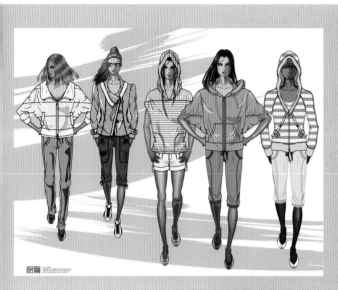

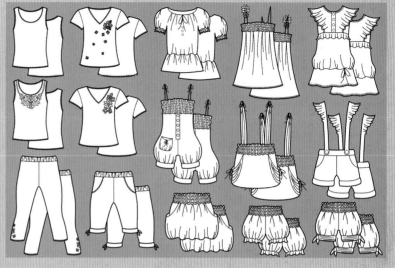

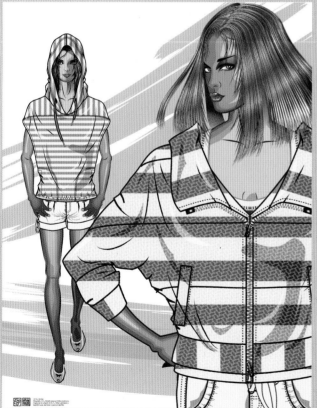

▲ SIMPLICITY
You don't have to include fabric swatches or working drawings on your board—sometimes it's best just to let the illustration speak for itself.

◄ HARMONY
Working drawings on figures allow for a more artistic depiction of the garments. A colored background can be effective. This one is blue and echoes tones used in the designs. Be careful that the color does not overwhelm the illustrations.

► WORK IN PROGRESS
Ideas in a sketchbook often have a liveliness that can be lost in a finalized work. If you plan to present a sketchbook, make sure it is neat and clean.

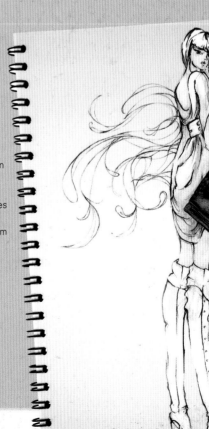

UNIT 24 Practicalities of presentation

Embellishing work with unnecessary extras can show a lack of confidence in the main concept, so whether you feel your designs call for an understated presentation or for a more elaborate themed approach, you must be sure that you don't include anything that does not contribute to the impact of the designs. You want someone seeing your illustrations for the first time to be struck by the quality of your design statement—not by the decoration surrounding it. A simple presentation has more chance of being successful, and will not offend anyone's tastes, although a more creative presentation style can create a strong impact (see Unit 27, pages 150–153). Decoration such as edgings must never overwhelm the illustrations, and colored backgrounds should be used only if they complement the design palette. Include items such as working drawings and swatches if they add to the clarity of the presentation, and remember that your work should appear clean and tidy.

Do not use spray adhesive to stick your images to the board, as this can cause respiratory damage. Dry-mounting images is a safer technique that involves placing a sheet of adhesive backing onto an illustration and then heating in order to adhere

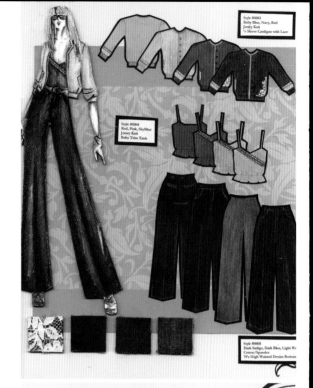

the project
Select a few of your favorite illustrations from the same project to mount on a 20 x 30-in. (50 x 75-cm) light foam board or boards. Don't worry about achieving a very dramatic style: this unit is about practicing well-organized, tidy, and effective presentation. Include items like fabric swatches if you wish, so long as the images are not obscured. You should choose and arrange your illustrations to reinforce the impression that they are part of a cohesive collection.

the objective
- Include items that contribute to the impact of your designs.
- Create a professional presentation.
- Present designs in a way that makes them look like part of a cohesive collection.

the process
Select a few designs to present from the same project. Before mounting, you may want to crop them to remove tattered edges or make the composition more focused. Use a scalpel and ruler or a guillotine. Clean up any smudge marks with a soft eraser.

Reproducing illustrations in a different medium may give a more professional finish, so consider taking photographs or making photocopies. You could even scan the pictures into a computer in order to further manipulate the designs, and then print the results.

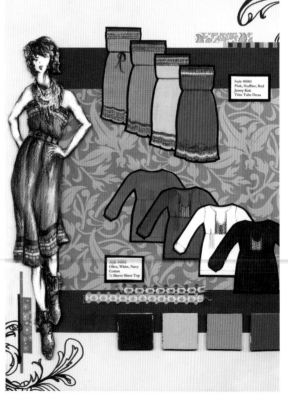

▶▲ CLEAR AND COHESIVE PRESENTATION
The deliberate use of colored background, swatches, and illustrations in these two examples help to show the cohesion within the ranges.

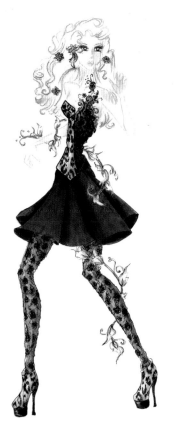

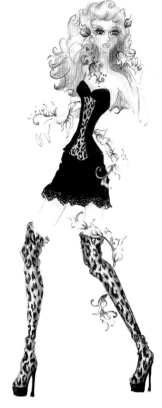

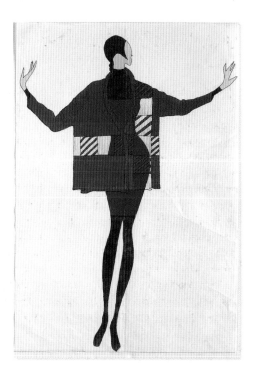

▶ STRONG STATEMENT
This bold design is best presented in a confident, understated way—there's no need for swatches, working drawings, edgings, or any other embellishment.

◀ REPEATING THE MOTIFS
These illustrations carry the theme's motif beyond the figure. The presentation emphasizes the cohesion of the collection through the use of a repeated dramatic pose.

Drawings that have been made using charcoal or pastel will smudge if they are not treated. Spray them with a fixative according to the instructions on the can. For health reasons, it is best to spray outside.

Never sign your illustrations as if they were finished works of art. However good they are, your drawings are not ends in themselves but commercial representations of ideas for garments.

You can mount your work straight onto the board or stick down a sheet of thin card as backing first. One (expensive) option is to cover the board with handmade paper with ragged edges and then mount straight-edged illustrations on top of that. Alternatively, you could use a board exactly the same size as the illustration, so that no background shows at all. Resist trying to be too clever with your mounts. A controlled use of borders can help to give a more defined presentation, but if in any doubt keep it simple, or avoid them altogether. Colored paper can work as a backing for designs in a complementary palette, but be careful that the use of color does not detract from the image itself.

You don't want to overload your board, but clarity can be added with items such as fabric swatches (if your textile is complicated, it is better to display the detail with a small sample rather than trying to capture it in the garment drawing) and flat working drawings.

Decide how many illustrations you want to include on the board and, before sticking anything down, arrange all the illustrations and other items. Don't try to cram on too much information and don't overlap the illustrations so much that you can't see the designs. If you are presenting on more than one board, you can repeat color and composition to give the group a cohesive feel. Start sticking down the images only when you are happy with the overall composition. The easiest way of attaching items to a board is by using adhesive stick or peel-off double-sided mounts. Peel-off mounts make removing images simpler if you decide to remount them.

SEE ALSO
● Choosing a presentation style, p. 144
● Presenting with flair, p. 150

SELF-CRITIQUE
● Is your presentation bold and not too busy?
● Is the work neat and clean?
● Will a viewer understand the design

UNIT 24 Practicalities of presentation

the image to the board. However, this is a laborious process, and it is simpler and quicker to use an adhesive stick or double-sided mounts.

The images featured here demonstrate that effective presentations can be either boldly simple—featuring only the garment itself and focusing on color and silhouette rather than on detail—or complex, incorporating fabric details, for example, that may be as prominent as the garment itself. Much depends on personal taste as well as on the nature of the garment: if the interest of a piece lies in the textile, then the portrayal of this aspect will be important. There are certain ground rules, however, that apply to every type of presentation. They should be strongly composed (as here), with the viewer's attention drawn immediately to the central concept—whether that is a jacket, a whole outfit, or a combination of fabric and garment. Presentations should also always be neat and clean, and give the impression that they have been professionally produced. Multiple presentations representing different pieces belonging to the same collection should be given cohesion through the repetition of aspects such as the composition, the use of color and decoration, and the positioning and pose of the figures.

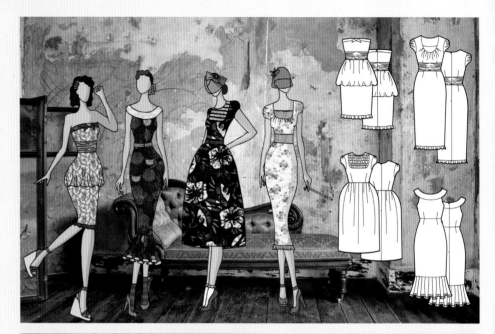

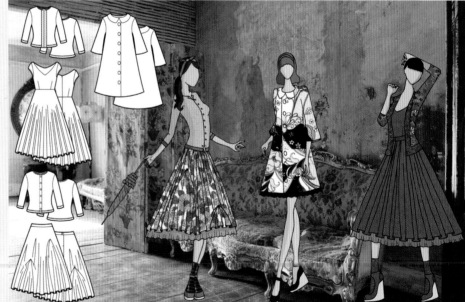

▲ **PRESENTING THE DETAILS**
As shown here, working drawings can add clarity to creative illustrations, and allow the details of the design to stand out.

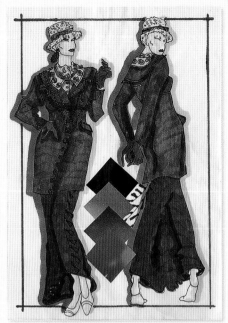

◀▼ USING BORDERS

Borders can be successfully used to add definition to a presentation. Illustrations can be framed within thin lines or wide edgings (as below), but this sort of decoration should only be applied if it does not diminish the impact of the design concept. Borders would seem too busy around a complicated print design, for example, which would be better presented on a plain white background.

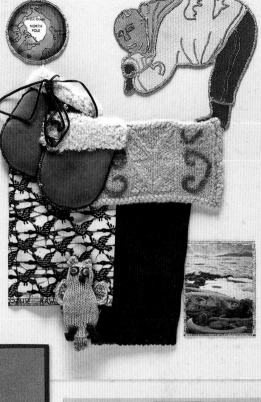

▼▶ COMPLEX BOARDS

Here, every item contributes to the design story—showing the texture of the fabric, the style of the garment, and its technical detail. Small examples of inspirational material can be included if, as here, they are not obtrusive and contribute to the mood of the piece.

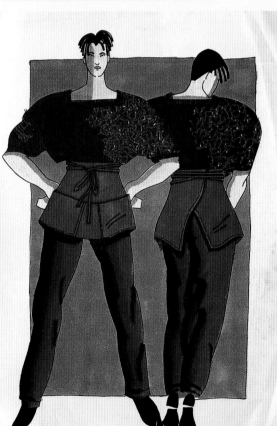

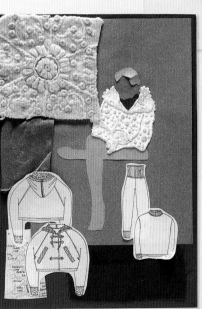

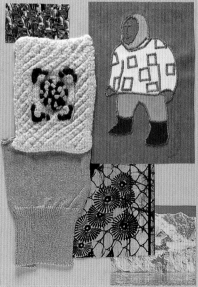

UNIT 25 Choosing a presentation style

Completing a number of presentation boards, each showing garments illustrated in a different style, will help you show off the versatility of your work to best advantage. This unit is intended to help you choose illustration styles that are appropriate for your designs and that will present them in their best light. You should choose a style of final illustration that both conveys your original inspiration and reinforces the design ideas, without taking over from the garments themselves. For example, if you have drawn inspiration from a natural source such as a shell, you might want to replicate its soft colors and delicate lines in your illustrations. You would also need to consider the nature of the garments themselves—neither a bold nor a painterly style would be suitable for illustrating a more conservative, commercial design. Try to use a different style of presentation for every project. By

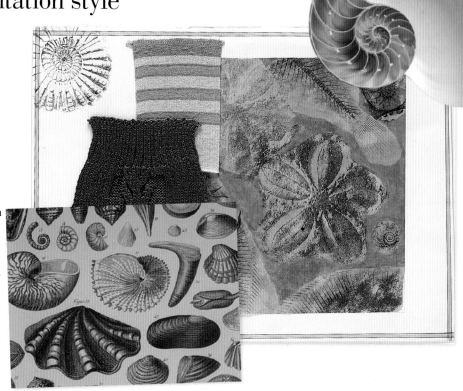

the project

Gather together inspirational research, mood boards, and rough sketches from some previous projects. Consider how appropriate the styles of drawing are to the original themes. Then experiment with different methods of illustration, inspired by your research and roughs. Support the designs with technical drawings, fabric swatches, and color swatches where appropriate.

the objective

● Assess critically the construction of existing garments.
● Draw designs in the method that shows them to best advantage.
● Challenge yourself by varying your presentation style.
● Create presentation boards that will give your portfolio impact and variety.

the process

Lay out all the elements of your chosen projects in a large space, including rough ideas, research material, and any mood boards. Place images side by side and compare the designs (if your work is in a sketchbook, photocopy the pages for this purpose). Reconsider the methods by which you have drawn (or intended to draw) your finished designs. The most appropriate illustration method will be closely tied to the level of detail that you need to show for each design.

If transparent layers are an important feature, illustrations might involve subtle color washes to suggest the see-through nature of the fabric. However, you would need to show more detail where garments include print or embroidery. It is not necessary to map out every stitch—this can be done on the flat working drawings (see Unit 22, pages 130–133)—but your

▲ FIRST INSPIRATIONS

Let your research guide you in choosing the most suitable method of illustrating your designs. An effective presentation goes beyond accurately depicting the garments: it sums up the whole mood of a collection. The fine lines and natural colors of these shell images might suggest a precise, delicate style, perhaps using watercolors or pen and ink.

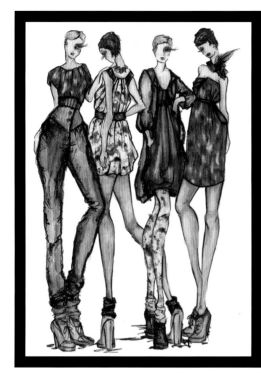

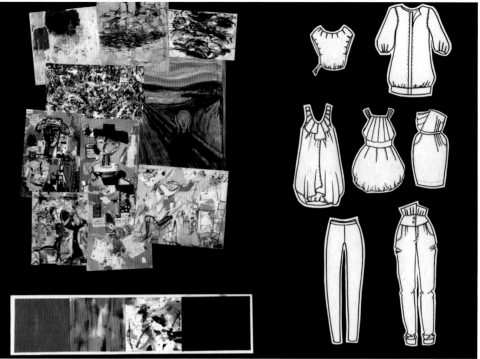

illustrations should show the scale and position of the decoration.

Look to your research for clues about the best style of illustration to depict your designs. A soft feminine theme might require a painterly approach, whereas a modern theme might find you scanning images into a computer and manipulating them with illustration software. Think creatively and aim to build up a varied set of styles within your portfolio to illustrate your flexibility and adaptability.

To communicate your design concept clearly (especially if your work is very painterly), consider including items such as working drawings, samples of fabrics or yarns, or even small examples of inspirational research material. Do not be tempted to overload the board with too much information, otherwise the clarity of the presentation will suffer.

▲ FOCUSED PRESENTATION STYLE
Think carefully about the mood that you are trying to convey. Dramatic designs can be communicated effectively in a bold style, whereas a more commercial look may demand a more traditional approach.

▶ A BALANCED STYLE
Remember to balance the creative effect of your presentation style with the need to accurately represent the fit of the garments and the textures of the fabrics.

SEE ALSO
- Clarity and communication, p. 128
- Presenting with flair, p. 150

SELF-CRITIQUE
- Have you successfully experimented with different styles of illustration and final presentation?
- Does the style of illustration show off each design in its best light?
- Have you achieved a balance between clarity and creativity?
- Do you have professional presentations to add to your portfolio?

UNIT 25 Choosing a presentation style

varying the flavor of each board, you will ensure that you build up a diverse body of work to appeal to a range of clients.

Designers vary their illustration style from project to project, building up a portfolio that contains a range of presentations, each one telling a different story both in terms of design and style of presentation. This demonstrates versatility and ensures that each project has its own personality. The illustrations can be made using pen and ink, paint, collage, felt-tip pen, computer scanning—anything goes, so long as the illustration style contributes to the overall theme and communicates the designer's vision.

The creation of effective presentation boards is a detailed and time-consuming process. Plenty of time should be allowed: it is easy to get bogged down in the rough planning stage and end up rushing the final presentation, which will spoil the impact of the ideas when they are shown to potential clients or employers. A good presentation, like those illustrated here, displays the garments in a way that is attractive but also easy to interpret. The golden rule is simplicity. Items such as swatches, working drawings, and trims can be included so long as they add clarity rather than detract from the impact of the garment itself; they are not always necessary.

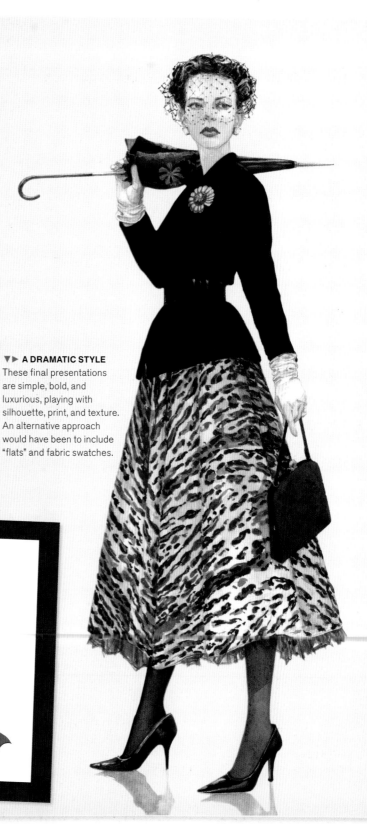

▼▶ **A DRAMATIC STYLE**
These final presentations are simple, bold, and luxurious, playing with silhouette, print, and texture. An alternative approach would have been to include "flats" and fabric swatches.

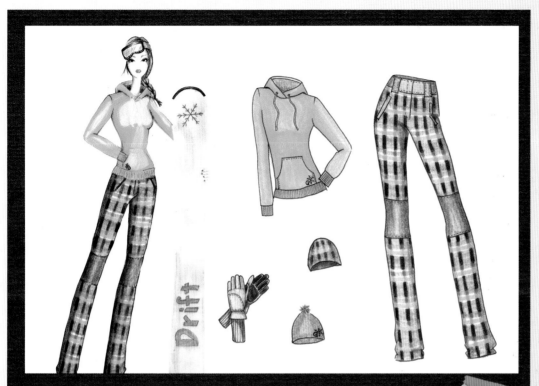

◄ AVOIDING AMBIGUITY
These creative illustrations are supported with flat technical drawings. The two styles of illustration support each other to give maximum clarity to the presentation.

► DEPICTING FABRICS
If original fabric designs are an important feature, samples should be included in the presentation. To avoid overwhelming illustrations of the garment silhouettes, the detail of the textiles could be displayed as swatches, either separately on the same board or on a different board.

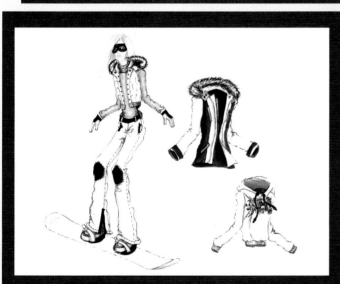

 ▲ HAVING FUN
An activewear range might inspire a light-hearted illustration style that is concerned with fun rather than realism.

UNIT 26 Digital portfolios

With the network of possible connections on the web, your designs and illustrations can reach people and places that they never have before. Once you have taken the time to learn about design and illustration, and produced some quality work, you can create digital portfolios on a variety of platforms to share your work. Always remember that your portfolio is only as good as your worst piece, so it's essential that you only share a small selection of your best, cleanest, and most professional pieces. Do not include every drawing and design you create; be very selective in the process, knowing that once you post something on the web, you can probably never retrieve all the copies of it.

There are a variety of ways to create and share your digital portfolio. For a limited or selective sharing process, a business card, or a group of related work samples, along with your contact information, saved in a PDF file, is sufficient.

PDF files

You can assemble about six of your best pieces and organize them in a PDF file that can then be saved on the hard drive. This digital portfolio can then be shared via E-mail or portable drives (CDs or flash drives) and devices (such as iPhones and iPads). What you include in your portfolio will depend on your purpose and target audience. If you aim to work for a men's clothing company, you would include men's designs. As your career develops, you will create multiple portfolios.

Getting your work online

To create a more open-source portfolio, you can use a variety of web storage options. If you are looking to share your work with a wide array of potential audiences, you can create a personal web site or post your work using a variety of web sources. You can buy a domain and create a personalized web site. This is the most costly option. You could also use a template-based web site that is geared toward showcasing art and design portfolios; some require a paid subscription, but many are free. Two great, free, template-based web spaces for fashion designers are *www.styleportfolios.com* and *www.coroflot.com*. On these sites you can not only post your work samples, but also reach a wider range of employers, who often search through these portfolios. Another option is the effective use of social networking and blogging sites such as Facebook and Google blogger; these are free and have the potential to reach a great number of people. Photo-sharing sites such as Flickr and Google's Picasa are also excellent resources, as your web albums from these sites can be incorporated into other supporting sites, such as blogs.

Important considerations

When making your digital portfolio in any format, consistency is the most important aspect of your creation. For example, if you are creating a PDF file of your portfolio, stay consistent with the size and orientation of the files. Keep them all horizontal, or all vertical, depending on your included pieces. Also

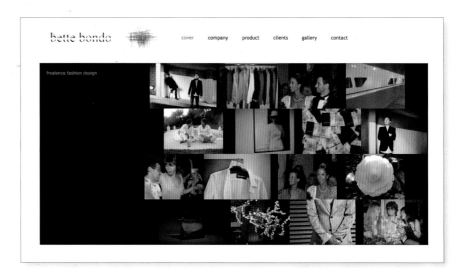

▲ **HOMEPAGE**
A multi-image homepage gives an overview of a company's diversity, and will make the viewer want to see more. A simple menu bar at the top provides easy links to pages of further interest.

SEE ALSO
● Digital presentation
  boards, p. 32

keep their dimensions the same—the size is not important as long as the digital canvases of the artwork/designs are consistent in size. This emphasis on consistency is to provide a uniform and uninterrupted visual flow. When publishing multiple forms of your portfolio, such as a business card, a CD-ROM, and a web site, it's a good idea to coordinate them all for recognition and consistency.

Overall, remember to keep the design of the site simple and skip the splash page—you don't want clients to leave before getting to the content. Make contact or E-mail links easy to read, and only use scripted fonts for headlines.

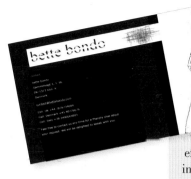

▲ **USING YOUR WEB IMAGES**
When designing web pages, consider how elements of the design could be incorporated into a business card.

Business cards

Most business cards don't stand out and end up being ignored. Making an effort to create a memorable business card will pay off. Don't scrimp on printing or effort. Take time to create a card with an interesting color, size, texture, and creative logo. A card that is trimmed a little smaller than a traditional card will stand out. Use a font that is easy to read. Keep it simple and mention only what you specialize in. Contact information is a must—it is surprising how many people forget this. Ask a friend or colleague to proofread the card, because when focused on the design, it's easy to miss a typo. Search web sites to see different designs and then locate the best printing options. Different techniques, such as die-cuts, specialty inks, and engravings, are all interesting options that should be explored. Make sure the card is small enough to fit into a wallet and doesn't appear too complicated.

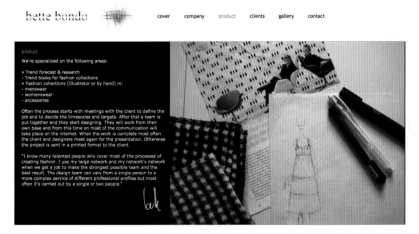

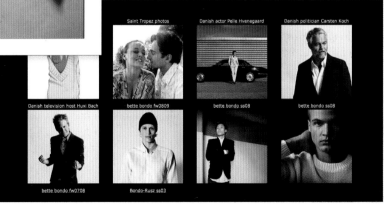

▲ **PRODUCT DESIGN**
Suitable imagery, and a simple but stylish design, informs the viewer of the company's expertise and work processes.

▶ **THE GALLERY**
Good photography and a simple layout provides the viewer with visual information. A quick click on the picture leads the viewer to new pages that highlight end products for key clients.

UNIT 26 Presenting with flair

While it is true that you should not overpresent your work so that the style of presentation becomes more powerful than the content, you should also not be impeded by the need for clear and simple presentation. If you maintain a careful balance, a creative presentation will add to the overall impact of your design project. This unit is intended to maximize your creativity in presentation—encouraging you to think not only about your drawing style but also about the poses of the figures, the use of fabrics, colors, lettering, and decoration, the possibilities offered by different media, and the overall effect of the board. Your aim should be to channel all these aspects into the creation of presentations that will communicate your vision to colleagues, teachers, employers and clients.

Although it is important not to overembellish a presentation so that it has more impact than the

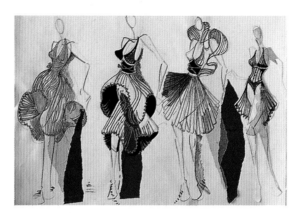

◀ ▶ **CREATING EXCITEMENT**
Even the pose of your figures can reflect your source. The "showgirl" stance of these figures reinforces the glamorous theme and lends a feeling of movement and celebration to the pictures.

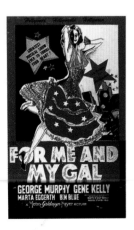
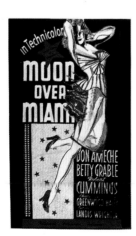

▲ **STRENGTHENING THE DESIGNS**
These presentation boards in the style of 1940s movie posters reinforce the impact of the glamorous tailoring of the designs themselves.

the project
Gather together all the elements of a previous design project. These will include the original sources of inspiration, your research, your sketchbook work, roughs, working drawings, final illustrations, and any photographs you may have taken. Considering this material and the nature of your design theme, and your target audience, decide on the most appropriate method of final presentation. Pick out your key designs and present them in a manner that supports and promotes your fashion ideas.

the objective
Create original presentation boards that reflect your unique style.
● Strengthen the impact of your design ideas by using complementary presentation methods.
● Tailor your presentation to your target audience.
● Balance the clear communication of your ideas with exciting and creative methods of presentation.

the process
Find a large table or a clean floor space that will allow you to lay out lots of images. Group them together so that you are able to see your initial inspiration, roughs, and

final illustrations side by side. Take a critical look at your developments. What was it that attracted you to this topic, and how have you expanded upon these ideas as you worked on the project? Is the theme still strongly reflected or have your designs evolved away from your starting point? Start to identify elements that could be used for presentation, such as interesting motifs, color combinations, textures, styles of lettering, garment styling ideas, methods of photography, and types of paper.

Decide on how you want to present your ideas. If your work has a glamorous feel inspired by

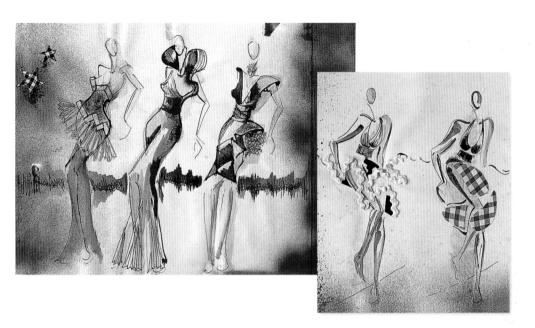

movie stars, your drawings could be supported with some exciting photography styles, perhaps using dramatic lighting or black and-white film. Do not slavishly copy existing styles, no matter how authentic they are to your research, but reinvent your inspiration in a modern context.

Always ask yourself whether potential clients will be able to relate to your methods of presentation. Buyers working in a commercial arena might be alienated by a very dramatic style of presentation, whereas a client with whom you are working on a bridal collection will have a romantic expectation of both the designs and the style of presentation.

Remember that you are trying to achieve a balance between communicating your design concepts with clarity and creating a visually exciting presentation. You should also choose a style of illustration appropriate to your theme (see Unit 25, pages 144–147). Make sure that the arrangement on your board is not overcrowded (for some useful practical tips see Unit 24, pages 140–143). If necessary, prioritize garment illustrations, working drawings, and fabric swatches.

▼ REINFORCING YOUR IDEAS
The dramatic approach of this "showgirl" theme is reinforced through the choice of silhouette, fabric, and styling. The presentation style can aid the impact of drawings by echoing colors and design elements.

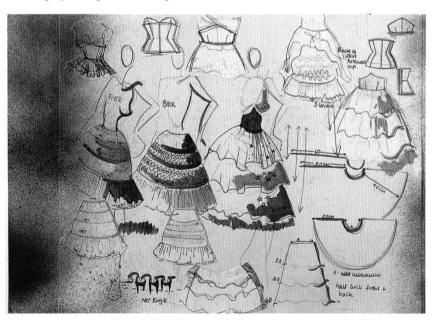

UNIT 27 Presenting with flair

garment designs themselves, a carefully prepared presentation will strengthen the illustrations. These presentations underline the glamour of designs based on the worlds of film and theater in various ways. Dramatic photography and the use of a billboard poster style suggest a movie-star theme, and sketches reminiscent of costume design, the use of spray paint and star motifs, and the portrayal of showgirl fabrics like satin, boned silk, diamanté embroideries, and feathers evoke the theater. Marilyn Monroe's famous billowing-skirt pose is reproduced in one set of drawings; in another, Judy Garland's ruby slippers add a witty touch. If stuck for ideas when presenting designs, think back to the original source. Garments inspired by a beautiful garden, for example, might well be photographed laid on flowers or hanging among branches. So long as the presentation supports the designs, there is always opportunity to be creative.

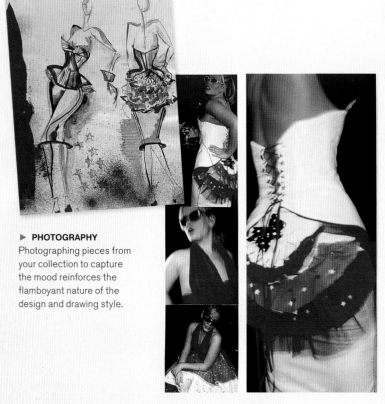

▶ **PHOTOGRAPHY**
Photographing pieces from your collection to capture the mood reinforces the flamboyant nature of the design and drawing style.

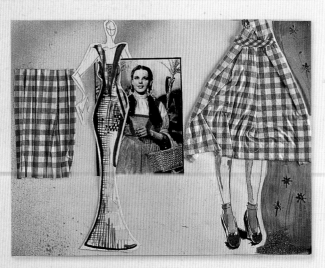

▲ ▶ **EVOKING THE INSPIRATION**
The fabric used here was inspired by *The Wizard of Oz*.

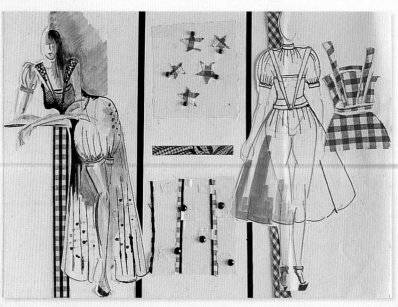

▶ ▼ RESTATING THE SOURCE

The Marilyn Monroe-style poses of these illustrations support the cinematic theme wonderfully, adding authority to the concept.

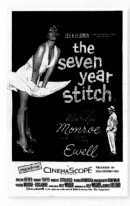

Coordinated Sketchbook

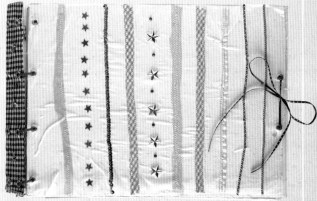

▶ PRESENTING A SKETCHBOOK

Even the cover of this sketchbook was embellished to coordinate with the design story.

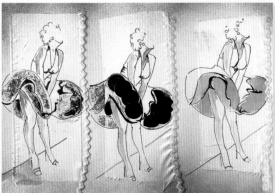

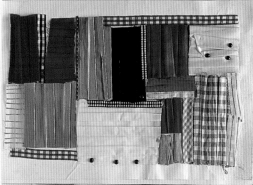

◀ ▼ ELABORATING ON THE DETAILS

Fabrics, trims, and other details can make great presentation ideas—used as an edging on a board, perhaps, or to decorate the cover of a sketchbook—so long as they do not detract from the designs.

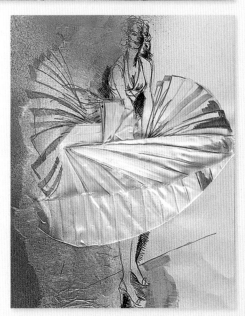

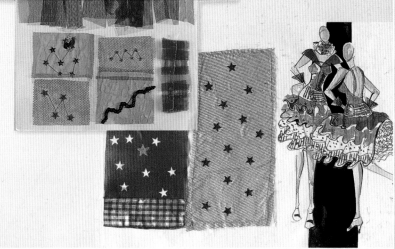

Fashion resources

Courses in fashion design

The following list comprises only a very small selection of the many colleges and universities worldwide with departments of fashion design. Whether you are looking for an evening class or for full-time study in an undergraduate or postgraduate program, the huge variety of options available should mean that you have no problem in finding the course that's right for you.

AUSTRALIA

Royal Melbourne Institute of Technology
G.P.O. Box 2476
Melbourne
Victoria 3001
t.: (+61) 3 9925 2000
www.rmit.edu.au

CANADA

Academy of Arts and Design
2nd floor, 7305 Marie Victorin
Brossard
Quebec J4W 1A6
t.: (+1) 514 875 9777
www.aadmtl.com

Montreal Superior Fashion School
LaSalle College
2000 Ste-Catherine St. W.
Montreal
Quebec H3H 2T2
t.: (+1) 514 939 2006
www.lasallecollege.com

DENMARK

Copenhagen Academy of Fashion Design
Nørrebrogade 45, 1. sal
2200 Copenhagen N.
t.: (+45) 33 328 810
www.modeogdesignskolen.dk

FRANCE

Creapole
128 rue de Rivoli
75001 Paris
t.: (+33) 1 4488 2020
www.creapole.fr

Esmod/Isem Paris
12 rue de la Rochefoucauld
75009 Paris
t.: (+33) 1 4483 8150
www.esmod.com

Parsons Paris
14 rue Letellier
75015 Paris
t.: (+33) 1 4577 3966
www.parsons-paris.pair.com

ITALY

Domus Academy
Via G. Watt 27
20143 Milano
t.: (+39) 2 4241 4001
www.domusacademy.it

Polimoda
Via Pisana 77
50143 Florence
t.: (+39) 55 739 961
www.polimoda.com

NETHERLANDS

Amsterdam Fashion Institute
Amstelgebouw
Mauritskade 11
1091 GC Amsterdam
t.: (+31) 20 525 67 77
www.international.hva.nl/schools/school-of-design-and-communication

SPAIN

Institucion Artistica de Enseñanza
c. Claudio Coello 48
28001 Madrid
t.: (+34) 91 577 17 28
www.iade.es

UNITED KINGDOM

University of Brighton
Mithras House
Lewes Road
Brighton BN2 4AT
t.: (+44) (0)1273 600 900
www.brighton.ac.uk

**Central St. Martin's College of
Art and Design**
Southampton Row
London WC1B 4AP
t.: (+44) (0)20 7514 7022
www.csm.linst.ac.uk

De Montfort University
The Gateway
Leicester LE1 9BH
t.: (+44) (0)116 255 1551
www.dmu.ac.uk

Kingston University
River House
53–57 High Street
Kingston upon Thames
Surrey KT1 1LQ
t.: (+44) (0)20 8417 9000
www.kingston.ac.uk

University of Lincoln
Admissions & Customer Services
Brayford Pool
Lincoln LN6 7TS
t.: (+44) (0)1522 882 000
www.lincoln.ac.uk

London College of Fashion
20 John Princes Street
London W1G 0BJ
t.: (+44) (0)20 7514 7400
www.lcf.linst.ac.uk

University of the Arts London
272 High Holborn
London WC1V 7EY
t.: (+44) (0)20 7514 6000
www.linst.ac.uk

University of Manchester
Oxford Road
Manchester M13 9PL
t.: (+44) (0)16 1306 6000
www.manchester.ac.uk

Nottingham Trent University
Burton Street
Nottingham NG1 4BU
t.: (+44) (0)115 941 8418
www.ntu.ac.uk

Ravensbourne
6 Penrose Way
London SE10 0EW
t.: (+44) (0)20 3040 3500
www.rave.ac.uk

Royal College of Art
Kensington Gore
London SW7 2EU
t.: (+44) (0)20 7590 4444
www.rca.ac.uk

**University for the Creative Arts
at Farnham**
Falkner Road
Farnham
Surrey GU9 7DS
t.: (+44) (0)1252 722 441
www.ucreative.ac.uk

UNITED STATES

**American InterContinental University
(Buckhead)**
3330 Peachtree Road N.E.
Atlanta, GA 30326
t.: (+1) 800 955 2120
www.aiuniv.edu/Atlanta/

**American InterContinental University
(Los Angeles)**
12655 W. Jefferson Blvd
Los Angeles, CA 90066
t.: (+1) 888 594 9888
www.la.aiuniv.edu

Cornell University
Campus Information and Visitor Relations
Day Hall Lobby
Cornell University
Ithaca, NY 14853
www.cornell.edu

Fashion Careers of California College
1923 Morena Blvd
San Diego, CA 92110
t.: (+1) 619 275 4700
www.fashioncareerscollege.com

**Fashion Institute of Design &
Merchandising (FIDM) (Los Angeles)**
919 S. Grand Avenue
Los Angeles, CA 90015-1421
t.: (+1) 800 624 1200
www.fidm.com

**Fashion Institute of Design &
Merchandising (FIDM) (San Diego)**
350 Tenth Avenue, 3rd Floor
San Diego, CA 92101
t.: (+1) 619 235 2049
www.fidm.com

**Fashion Institute of Design &
Merchandising (FIDM) (San Francisco)**
55 Stockton Street
San Francisco, CA 94108-5829
t.: (+1) 415 675 5200
www.fidm.com

Fashion Institute of Design and Merchandising (Orange County)
17590 Gillette Avenue
Irvine, CA 92614-5610
t.: (+1) 949 851 6200
www.fidm.com

Fashion Institute of Technology
Seventh Avenue at 27th Street
New York, NY 10001-5992
t.: (+1) 212 217 7999
www.fitnyc.edu

International Academy of Design and Technology (Chicago)
1 North State Street, Suite 400
Chicago, IL 60602
t.: (+1) 312 980 9200
www.iadt.edu/Chicago

International Academy of Design and Technology (Tampa)
5104 Eisenhower Blvd
Tampa, FL 33634
t.: (+1) 813 699 5206
www.iadt.edu/Tampa

Parsons The New School for Design
66 Fifth Avenue
New York, NY 10011
t.: (+1) 212 229 8900
www.parsons.edu

School of Fashion Design
136 Newbury Street
Boston, MA 02116
t.: (+1) 617 536 9343
www.schooloffashiondesign.org

College of Visual Arts and Design
1155 Union Circle #305100
Denton, TX, 76203-5017
t.: (+1) 940 565 2855
www.art.unt.edu

Fashion designers online

If you are stuck for inspiration or want to bring yourself up to date on forthcoming trends, why not check out the web sites belonging to the top fashion designers? Here are just some of the good sites:

www.agnesb.fr
www.alexandermcqueen.co.uk
www.annasui.com
www.antoniandalison.co.uk
www.apc.fr
www.balenciaga.com
www.betseyjohnson.com
www.bless-service.de
www.bruunsbazaar.com
www.burberry.com
www.calvinkleininc.com
www.celine.com
www.chanel.com
www.christian-lacroix.fr
www.coupny.com
www.daniellenault.com
www.delphinepariente.fr
www.dior.com
www.dolcegabbana.it
www.donnakaran.com
www.driesvannoten.be
www.dvf.com
www.elspethgibson.com
www.emiliopucci.com
www.fendi.it
www.ghost.co.uk
www.gianfrancoferre.com
www.giorgioarmani.com
www.giovannivalentino.com
www.givenchy.com
www.gucci.com
www.helmutlang.com
www.hugo.com
www.isseymiyake.com
www.jaeger-lecoultre.com
www.jasperconran.com
www.johngalliano.com

www.jpgaultier.fr
www.karenwalker.com
www.katespade.com
www.kennethcole.com
www.kenzo.com
www.lacoste.com
www.lloydklein.com
www.lucienpellat-finet.com
www.marcjacobs.com
www.michaelkors.com
www.michikokoshino.co.uk
www.moschino.it
www.oscardelarenta.com
www.pacorabanne.com
www.patriciafield.com
www.paulsmith.co.uk
www.peopleusedtodream.com
www.polo.com
www.prada.com
www.redblu.com
www.robertocavalli.it
www.rodarte.net
www.seanjohn.com
www.soniarykiel.com
www.stellamccartney.com
www.tommy.com
www.versace.com
www.viviennewestwood.co.uk
www.vuitton.com
www.yohjiyamamoto.co.jp
www.ysl.com

Glossary

"all-ways" print A print with motifs that are not aligned in any one particular direction: the fabric will work in the same way whichever way up it is.

art deco A design style, popular between the two World Wars, that was characterized by simplicity, bold outlines, geometrical order, and the use of new materials such as plastic.

bias cutting Cutting fabric with the pattern pieces placed at a 45-degree angle to the selvages and the grain.

brief The client's, employer's, or tutor's instructions to a designer, setting the parameters of a design project.

clip-art images Copyright-free images available through the Internet.

collage An image created by sticking items (such as paper cuttings or pieces of cloth) to a surface. From the French **coller** ("to glue").

collection The group of garments produced each season by a designer. Usually these items have certain features in common, such as color, shape, and pattern.

color palette A limited selection of colors used by a designer when creating a collection to ensure a cohesive color scheme.

color theming Giving the items in a collection a common identity through the repeated use of certain colors.

colorway The choice of colors used in an individual piece. Changing the colorway can alter the look of a garment dramatically.

cropping Trimming an illustration to alter the focus of the composition or to remove tattered edges.

customer profile Information about the lifestyle of the target customer—such as age, economic status, and occupation—that guides a designer in creating commercially viable collections.

dry-mounting Placing adhesive backing onto an illustration and then heating in order to adhere it to a board.

grain The fabric grain is the direction of the woven fibers, either lengthwise or crosswise. Most dressmaking pieces are cut on the lengthwise grain, which has minimal stretch; when bias cutting, pieces are placed diagonally to the grain.

layout The composition of the illustration on the page. A bold layout, which fills the page and makes the design statement with confidence, is often the most successful approach.

mixed media A combination of different media within the same image. Possible media include color pencils, oil pastels, crayons, gouache, watercolor paints, pen and ink, or even a computer or photocopier.

mood board A board displaying inspirational research, current fashion images, fabric swatches, and color palettes. It should encapsulate the most important themes from the research and act as a focus during the creation of the designs.

"negative space" Part of the illustration left deliberately blank so that viewers, who might have expected these areas to be filled in, will read the invisible lines through the white space.

"one-way" print A print where the motifs are aligned in one direction. More expensive to use for making garments than "all-ways" prints because extra fabric is required to align the print correctly.

Pantone color chips Individually numbered shades, supplied in color reference books. The numbered shades are recognized throughout the international fashion industry.

portfolio A case used for storing, transporting, and displaying illustrations.

presentation board A light foam board available in various sizes from art supply stores. Used for presenting work to tutors, employers, and clients.

range Used interchangeably with "collection" to describe the group of garments produced each season by a designer. "Range" has also more specifically commercial overtones, indicating a selection of coordinating garments that offers maximum choice to the customer within the parameters of the range.

roughs The quick, unconstrained sketches that a designer uses to "think out loud on paper," developing a research idea into a range of designs.

silhouette The outline shape of a complete ensemble.

target customer The person who is likely to wear the designs produced for each project. A designer should construct a profile of the target customer in order to ensure that the garments are commercially focused.

target market The range of target customers that a retailer aims to satisfy.

working drawing The representation of a garment as it would look laid out flat rather than drawn on a figure. Used to convey precise information about the construction, trims, finishes, and any other details of the pieces. Also known as "flats," or technical or specification drawings.

Index

Credits

Quarto would like to thank the following for supplying images for inclusion in this book:

Alice Lam p.1, 11, 139b, 140, 145
Rachel Lerro www.rachellerro.com p.2, 96b, 110
Christine Lynch p.4, 5;
Nanae Taka p.6, 7, 70, 71
Jemi p.16, 17, 19, 21, 26br, 51, 52, 54, 55, 56,
    58, 60, 61, 62, 63, 64, 65, 66, 82, 83, 85tr,
    86–87 (fabric swatch illustrations), 88, 89, 100,
    101, 103tr/br, 125, 129b, 146bl/br
Photography Lorrie Ivas, p.16, 17, 86, 87
Timothy Lee p.23,24,25
Caroline Tatham p.27tc, 29, 30, 31, 46br, 48, 49,
    92tr,b, 93l, 94, 95, 96bl, 97, 99, 104, 105, 106,
    107, 112, 113, 118, 119, 120, 121, 123, 130, 131,
    132bl,bc, 133, 134, 135, 136, 137, 143, 144
Wynn Armstrong p.32–33 (digital images), 35tl,
    78–79 (digital collage), 125 (digital trend
    board); Model Tanya Clarke p. 32, 33
James Warner p.34tr
Angela Chuy p.34b
Freida Lindstrom p.36tr
Nicole O'Malley www.nicoleomalley.com p.36bl, 59
Medha Khosla (front cover) p.37, 127
Sherina Dalarmal p.40, 41
Gamma/Simon-Stevens p.42t
Julian Seaman p.44, 45, 67, 77
Bridgeman p.52tr
Wikipedia p.53tl
Christine Mayes p.68
Casey Kresler p.69bl,c,r
Tara Al-Wali www.taraalwali.com p.75, 132tl,r
Clara Yoo (Parsons) p. 85
Getty Images p.91
Eri Wakiyama http://eithemermaid.blogspot.
    com p.111
Lan Nyguen p.108br, 111l

Tawana Walker p.117t
Holly Marler p.124, 150, 151, 152, 153
Tracy Turnbull p.137
Oksana Nedavniaya p.138tr, 146r
Josephine Brase www.brasedesign.com p.138
Chi Hu p.139t,b
Schuyler Hames p.139tr, 142
Julie McMurry p.141, 147bl
Joyce Iacoviello p.147t
Hyunju Park (Ck) p.147br
Bette Bondo www.bettebondo.com p.148,149